HOW MANY MACHINE GUNS DOES IT TAKE
TO COOK ONE MEAL?

HOW MANY MACHINE GUNS

DOES IT TAKE

TO COOK ONE MEAL?

THE SEATTLE AND
SAN FRANCISCO
GENERAL STRIKES

VICTORIA JOHNSON

A SAMUEL AND ALTHEA STROUM BOOK

UNIVERSITY OF WASHINGTON PRESS SEATTLE AND LONDON

THIS BOOK IS PUBLISHED WITH THE ASSISTANCE OF A GRANT
FROM THE SAMUEL AND ALTHEA STROUM ENDOWED BOOK FUND.

University of Washington Press
PO Box 50096, Seattle, WA 98145
www.washington.edu/uwpress

Library of Congress Cataloging-in-Publication Data
Johnson, Victoria L. (Victoria Lee)
How many machine guns does it take to cook one meal? : the Seattle and San
Francisco General Strikes / Victoria Johnson.
p. cm.
Includes bibliographical references and index.
ISBN 978-0-295-98796-5 (hardback : alk. paper)
1. General Strike, Seattle, Wash., 1919.   2. General Strike, San Francisco, Calif.,
1934.   3. Strikes and lockouts—United States—History—20th century.   4. Working
class—United States—History—20th century.   5. Labor movement—United States—
History—20th century.   I. Title.   II. Title: Seattle and San Francisco General Strikes.
HD5326.W2J64 2007   331.892'5097946109044—DC22   2007038317

IN MEMORY OF VIRGINIA JOHNSON,
AND FOR MY CAT, MR. "FURRY" BRIDGES

CONTENTS

PREFACE

When I was a graduate student in Northern California, I learned that general strikes had taken place in the United States. I was both intrigued and puzzled. General strikes occur when organized labor shuts down industries crucial to the functioning of cities or regions. Yet much of the existing literature on the topic has characterized American labor as politically conservative and, for lack of a better term, as consisting of "capitalist wannabes." Proponents of American exceptionalism have long argued that there is something different about U.S. culture and its institutions that fosters conservatism in contrast to "class-conscious" Europeans, who have identified with socialist and communist challenges to capitalism. Although excellent research has documented numerous examples of labor radicalism throughout American history, the consensus is that by the twentieth century most Americans had accepted capitalism. My personal experiences at various jobs over the years—as a salesperson, printer's apprentice, casino employee, newspaper inserter, and staff member in a women's health clinic—have led me to agree with this consensus.

How, then, do we explain Americans participating in general strikes, the most insurrectionary tactic short of revolt? At least twenty general strikes have taken place in the United States, the vast majority of them occurring in the first half of the twentieth century. Given the conservative characterizations of American labor, however, I wondered what conditions elicited these great strikes and, of particular importance, how did Americans justify shutting down entire cities? Did culture, whether conservative or class-conscious, play a role? I set about to answer these questions through a historical and comparative analysis of the general strikes in Seattle in 1919 and in San Francisco in 1934. This book is the result of that quest.

As I began my research, it became clear that increased union density, workplace organization, social and economic instability, and state actors and policies were important conditions in the emergence of these general strikes. Identifying such conditions was not surprising, given that most studies of the general strikes in Seattle and San Francisco have relied heavily on the institutional organization of the workplace, political power, and access to resources as explanatory devices. Yet as I continued to study the historical documents about these two cases, one thing stood out. The models of social change proposed by labor organizers during the precipitating strikes, out of which the general strikes emerged, seemed neither conservative nor class-conscious in the European manner. Mobilization appeals in Seattle emphasized the rights of labor to ownership and control of industries; those in San Francisco emphasized worker control of the hiring hall and rank-and-file control of the union. In both cases the emphasis on local democratic control of the workplace was prioritized in contrast to socialist or communist models of change, or at least as we understand them today as centralized state command economies.

Some scholars have attributed the orientations among labor in the San Francisco case to diffuse syndicalist tendencies among West Coast maritime workers, related in part to the impact of the anarcho-syndicalist Industrial Workers of the World (IWW). Anarcho-syndicalism, or what has been loosely called syndicalism in the literature, was an early-twentieth-century European orientation that rejected centralized state authority and sought direct control of industries by the unions or *syndicats* that worked in them. Seattle was a notable stronghold for the IWW during the second decade of the twentieth century. All right, I thought, the link to European syndicalism through the IWW explains the "radicalism" of labor during these general strikes.

But as I continued my sociological journey through the wonderland of labor history, I soon discovered links between the IWW and the Knights of Labor. The Knights was one of the last organizations of what has been called the labor movement for the self-governing workshop, which spanned the nineteenth century. This movement was dedicated to maintaining worker ownership and control of the workplace in response to escalating labor disempowerment that was occurring through the process of capitalist industrialization. These organizations proposed a variety of remedies for reclaiming workplace control, from land redistribution and laws against land monopolies to national industrial cooperatives. The labor movement for the self-governing workshop drew on early-nineteenth-century artisan republican vocabularies, with frequent references to Thomas Jefferson and Thomas Paine. My historical travels were thus coming to an end with one final destination—the early republic.

Like many Americans I thought the framers were mostly interested in private property rights and personal profit, and although they had great ideas about freedom and equality, they were exploitative in their practices toward women, African Americans, and indigenous populations. Some of these presumptions are accurate, but I was astounded when I looked more closely at the early republic, especially at the moral and political philosophies of Jefferson and Paine. Through their visions of what constituted a republic—including state distribution of land or money to its citizens as well as a political and workplace sovereignty secured through widely distributed property ownership—I began to understand in a different way the emphasis on property rights in American political history.

A model of an egalitarian republic emerged through the writings of Jefferson and Paine that exhibited continuities with the models of social change proposed by nineteenth-century labor organizations for the self-governing workshop. Initially this model applied only to Euro-American male landowners, but by the early nineteenth century contradictions between rhetoric and practice generated movements that expanded the model to include Euro-American male artisans and eventually people of color and women.

Discursive strands and practices reminiscent of the movement for the self-governing workshop were still apparent within labor cultures in Seattle in 1919 and in San Francisco in 1934. These vocabularies provided the moral justification for activists to mobilize labor to demand workplace control and to participate in general strikes. The movement for the self-governing workshop's vision of an egalitarian republic was different from socialism; although it was built on private-property ownership, it challenged many of today's neoliberal economic policies that disempower labor and facilitate the concentration of wealth and power.

Yet the self-governing workshop's vocabularies and models of social change have at times been constructed as "agrarian," "backwards looking," even "reactionary." They have largely been dismissed by scholars and activists as irrelevant to industrial or postindustrial societies.

This book invites the reader to rethink the American exceptionalism debate. Instead of being concerned with whether or to what extent American labor was class-conscious in the European manner, this work invites a rethinking of the models of economic and political change that have been considered *not* class-conscious. I seek to demonstrate that the movement for the self-governing workshop did not die out at the end of the nineteenth century. Not only did this movement's discursive strands and practices manifest themselves in Seattle in 1919 and in San Francisco in 1934, but they continue to resonate today, providing an opportunity to frame proposals for labor empowerment in the twenty-first century that are embedded within American moral and political values.

Given the complexity of social life, a caveat is needed about the construction of history and the analysis of culture. In order to identify continuities among the movement for the self-governing workshop with political cultures during the general strikes in Seattle and San Francisco, the discursive strands and practices identified appear much more linear and compact than they actually were. These strands were embedded within amalgams of discourses and practices, and among labor organizations and within regions not examined in this book. Too often complexity is lost when constructing history to draw the reader's attention to specific aspects. It is my hope, however, that these weaknesses will be compensated for through this book's contribution to our understanding of American class identities.

This work could not have been done without the many institutions that provided historical documents about the general strikes: the University of Washington Libraries, Manuscript & Archives Division and Special Collections; the Bancroft Library at the University of California, Berkeley; and the International Longshoremen's and Warehousemen's Union (ILWU) Library in San Francisco.

There are many people I would like to thank, although any weaknesses in the book are mine alone. Foremost I am indebted to John Walton and Fred Block for their excellent suggestions for manuscript revision and support for this project over the years. I have been privileged to work with Janet Gouldner, executive editor of the journal *Theory and Society*, and to have her continuing support. I am grateful to Margaret Levi and Mieke Meurs for their comments on my article "The Cultural Foundation of Resources, the Resource Foundation of Political Cultures: Explaining the Outcomes of Two General Strikes," which was printed in the September 2000 issue of *Politics and Society*, excepts from which have been included in chapter four. Anonymous reviewers for the University of Washington Press provided extremely helpful suggestions that prompted me to reconsider arguments and improve the manuscript. Special thanks go to my colleagues at the University of Missouri–Columbia, Clarence Lo and David Brunsma, as well as to Jesse Lawson, Maureen Sullivan, and Lowell Johnson for reviewing chapters. I must also acknowledge the stellar assistance of graduate student Steve Bernard.

Going back to the early stages of my research, I am grateful to the very helpful Gene Vrana, ILWU librarian. And I would like to extend a posthumous acknowledgment to retired seaman Revels Cayton, whom I interviewed in San Francisco. In Seattle thanks go to retired longshoreman Martin Jugum and to historian Ron Magden, who has researched waterfront workers for years and who was kind enough to speak with me. The "Harry Bridges: Tradition of Dissent" conference at the University of Washington in 1994 provided a wealth of information. One last acknowledgment is for all the historians and sociologists whose labor I have built on to write this book.

ABBREVIATIONS

AFL   American Federation of Labor

ALU   American Labor Union

BCC   Brotherhood of the Cooperative Commonwealth

CIO   Congress of Industrial Organizations

CP   Communist Party

EFC   Emergency Fleet Corporation

IA   Industrial Association

ILA   International Longshoremen's Association

ILD   International Labor Defense

ILWU   International Longshoremen's and Warehousemen's
          Union

IWW   Industrial Workers of the World

JMSC   Joint Marine Strike Committee

Knights   Knights of Labor

MWIU   Marine Workers Industrial Union

NIRA   National Industrial Recovery Act

NLB   National Longshoremen's Board

NLU   National Labor Union

Populists Populist Party

SCLC   Seattle Central Labor Council

SFLC   San Francisco Labor Council

SLAB   Shipbuilding Labor Adjustment Board

SSC   Strike Strategy Committee

WCLU   Western Central Labor Union

WES   Waterfront Employers of Seattle

WEU   Waterfront Employers Union

WFM   Western Federation of Miners

HOW MANY MACHINE GUNS DOES IT TAKE
TO COOK ONE MEAL?

1 NEW WINE IN OLD BOTTLES

Rethinking American Exceptionalism

With the laborers of England generally, does not the moral coercion
of want subject their will as despotically to that of their employer, as
the physical constraint does the soldier, the seaman, or the slave?

— *Thomas Jefferson, 1814*

I have already established the principle, namely, that the earth, in its
natural uncultivated state was, and ever would have continued to be, the
common property of the human race; that in that state, every person would
have been born to property; and that the system of landed property, by
its inseparable connection with cultivation . . . has absorbed the property
of all those whom it has dispossessed, without providing, as ought to have
been done, an indemnification for that loss. . . . In advocating the case
of persons dispossessed, it is a right, and not a charity that I am pleading
for. . . . To create a national fund, out of which there shall be paid to every
person, when arrived at the age [of] twenty-one years, the sum of fifteen
pounds sterling, as a compensation in part, for the loss of his or her natural
inheritance, by introduction of the system of landed property.

— *Thomas Paine, 1795*

In 1919 wage laborers in Seattle resisted the "moral coercion"
described in the chapter epigraph by Jefferson. The "dispossessed,"
as Paine would call them, participated in a five-day general strike
that shut down industries crucial to the city's operation. The rank and
file decided to have the general strike while Seattle Central Labor Coun-

cil (SCLC) officials were away at a meeting in Chicago. At issue was the interference of a government agency, the Emergency Fleet Corporation (EFC), in the collective bargaining of Seattle's shipyard unions. During the general strike organized labor took control of the city's management, providing food to the citizenry, emergency services to hospitals, and a nonviolent labor "police force" composed of World War I veterans.

Fifteen years later the West Coast would experience another general strike, this time in Northern California. The San Francisco 1934 general strike was preceded by a coastwide maritime strike with leadership centered in that city. As riots and street fighting with the police escalated, three protestors were shot; two died. The riots, which began when city officials and employers used the police to "open the port" that longshoremen had struck for almost two months, lasted several days until the governor called in the National Guard. In response, a general strike was mobilized by rank-and-file strike leadership, but not until they had circumvented the control of American Federation of Labor (AFL) officials who opposed it. During the general strike some restaurants stayed open, and emergency hospital services and the transport of milk continued by permission of the strike committee. Organized labor also set up union-supervised food depots and provided a labor police force to resolve problems that arose among workers.

These two general strikes seem worlds away from the plight of labor today. For the past few decades the right has dramatically increased its political and cultural power in the United States. Neoliberalism, which equates human labor with commodities and places private profit over public interest, has become the "common sense" of too many Americans. The dominant explanation for this rightward shift has been that conservatives speak the language of the American people, including the working class, while most Americans do not identify with liberals and the left.[1] The argument that liberals and the left desire changes that lack public resonance is reminiscent of the American exceptionalism debate, which goes back to the early twentieth century.[2]

AMERICAN EXCEPTIONALISM

The belief that American workers (and American politics and culture in general) are different and more conservative than their counterparts in Europe has been termed "American exceptionalism."[3] Economist and labor historian Selig Perlman's early-twentieth-century writings are representative of this interpretation of American political culture.[4] Having observed differences among workers in Germany, Great Britain, Russia, and the United States, Perlman concluded that Americans identified with the middle class were "practical" and desired a "communism of opportunity" instead of the state ownership of industries.[5] He attributed the success of the politically moderate AFL to its triumph over an alternative labor movement for the "self-governing workshop" in the nineteenth century.

The proposals of activists and labor organizations for the self-governing workshop ranged from land redistribution and laws against land monopolies to worker-owned cooperatives for production and distribution. In contrast to European socialism, the self-governing workshop "needed no sponsoring from the outside. To the American worker, who hankered to be rid of the capitalist 'boss,' a cooperative 'self bossing' seemed almost as desirable as self employment [sic]."[6] In contrast, workers in Australia, Belgium, England, France, Italy, Spain, and former West Germany have often been characterized as class-conscious because of their challenges to capitalism and their affiliation with labor, socialist, and communist parties.

But if proponents of American exceptionalism are right, and American labor is more conservative, how do we explain labor's participation in such general strikes as those in Seattle and San Francisco? In fact, there have been twenty-one general strikes in U.S. history.[7] They include strikes in St. Louis (1877); New Orleans (1892); Philadelphia (1910); Springfield, Illinois (1917); Billings, Montana (1917); Kansas City, Kansas (1918); Waco, Texas (1918); Seattle (1919); San Francisco (1934); Minneapolis (1934); Terre Haute, Indiana (1935); Pekin, Illinois (1936); Wilmington, Delaware (1937); Lansing, Michigan (1937); with the last strikes occurring in 1946, in Stamford and Hartford, Connecticut; Houston; Rochester, New York; Lancaster, Pennsylvania; Camden, New Jersey; and Oakland.[8]

The most distinctive characteristic of general strikes is the transfer of power from employers and city officials to organized labor. This occurred during both the Seattle and San Francisco general strikes as labor shut down industries and provided essential municipal services. This dynamic makes general strikes the most insurrectionary tactic short of revolt; certainly they have occurred during revolutions. Yet most general strikes have been called to obtain reformist rather than revolutionary goals.[9] Does the occurrence of American general strikes mean that their participants were class-conscious, as Europeans were? Some scholars disagree that American labor is exceptional. Instead, they have argued that the rank and file has often engaged in protests similar to the class-conscious struggles in Europe. These scholars tend to downplay political culture as important to labor insurrections and outcomes, focusing mostly on structural conditions, the organization of production, class formation, access to resources, and state facilitation or repression.[10]

What can general strikes tell us about the American exceptionalism debate? What conditions elicited these great strikes, and how were they justified by their participants? Was political culture, whether conservative or class-conscious, important at all? This book answers these questions through a historical and comparative analysis of general strikes in Seattle and San Francisco, but it is not exclusively about these strikes. Foremost, the book is about a *type* of political culture and its impact during collective action.

Most studies of general strikes have implicitly or explicitly drawn on structural determinist explanations.[11] This book recognizes the salience of economic and political conditions, as well as the constraints of institutional structures, but integrates culture into the fabric of analysis. Taking these strikes as case studies, we see how political culture was instrumental in their emergence, dynamics, and outcomes. But the political culture exhibited in each general strike cannot be characterized as either conservative or class-conscious in the European sense. Although socialists and communists were among labor factions that mobilized these strikes, their appeals did not promote a centralized state that owned the industries (the means of production) or directed the economy. Rather, the goals, strategies, and modes of organization exhibited by left labor factions more closely resembled the nineteenth-century labor movement for the self-governing workshop described earlier by Perlman. This alternative labor movement was informed by artisan republicanism, which drew inspiration from the moral and political philosophies of Thomas Jefferson and Thomas Paine.

We cannot conclude, however, as many scholars have, that these political roots signify that American labor was therefore conservative and accepting of capitalism. This book invites the reader to rethink the American exceptionalism debate, but not in terms of whether and to what degree American labor was class-conscious. Rather, it invites a rethinking of the models of economic and political change that scholars and activists alike have dismissed as lacking class consciousness. With some exceptions those scholars and activists have taken European class consciousness to be the authentic form of labor radicalism, comparatively relegating American labor to a negative case. But negative case comparisons frame the data in such a way as to obscure alternative explanations.[12] A type of distinctively American political culture was exhibited during these general strikes that challenged employer control and their "unjust accumulation" of wealth, and that resonated with American class identities. Identifying this political culture could be key to restoring discourses that legitimate labor empowerment in the United States.

TELEOLOGICAL DIVERSIONS

A small group of scholars are familiar with the early republic and the Jeffersonian and Paineite political theories that artisan republicanism drew on and that informed the labor movement for a self-governing workshop. Among its activists and organizations we find radical artisans like Langton Byllesby and Thomas Skidmore in the 1820s, Jacksonian Democrats in the 1830s, and the intellectual reformer George Evans and the cooperative movements of the 1840s and 1850s. By the 1860s the National Labor Union (NLU) had formed, with the Knights of Labor (hereafter the Knights) to follow in the later nineteenth century along with the agrarian-based Populist Party (hereafter the Populists). Their proposals for change differed, but their visions of a republic of labor exhibited common features—widely distributed wealth and political power among independent worker-owners. This vision was rooted in the rights of citizenship and can be inferred from Jefferson's and Paine's moral and political philosophies.[13]

Several interconnected discursive strands informed this vision of a republic. First was the commitment to civic virtue (or political integrity) that placed the public good over private interests. Second was the notion of "propertied independence," meaning that property ownership secured sovereignty over one's labor, and political beliefs. A third discursive strand was the moral imperative that labor creates wealth and those who labor have a right to the wealth they produce. These concepts were interwoven into various visions of a republic of labor, but all of these sprang from a common model different from socialism. Rather than having those who labor receive distributions of resources through state ownership of the means of production, Jefferson and Paine proposed that the state facilitate a wide distribution of resources to "citizens" to earn livelihoods through their "industry" and to secure their "political independence."

Yet the political and economic proposals of artisan republicanism and the movement for the self-governing workshop have been buried in history books along with the epithets "agrarian" and "backwards looking." It is presumed that artisan republican vocabularies became obsolete with industrialization. Labor scholar Gerald Grob, for example, has stated that the Knights flourished at a time when "the development of an industrial economy had not yet overwhelmed a predominantly rural nation . . . the Knights looked to the past rather than the future for their inspiration."[14] Given its "archaic" artisan republican vision, the labor movement for the self-governing workshop is presumed to have died in the late nineteenth century with the ascendancy of the "practical" trade unionism of the AFL.

This study of general strikes in Seattle and San Francisco reveals that, on the contrary, the labor movement for the self-governing workshop did not die out. West Coast activists and organizations continued some of the discursive strands and modes of organization of this movement into the twentieth century. Different waves of labor organizations emerged with robust economies and subsided with economic depressions, loss of strikes, and/or state repression. But clusters of narratives, practices, and collective identities continued in abeyance through activist networks for future generations to adopt.[15] Some activists left defunct labor organizations and joined new ones, bringing political philosophies and tactical repertoires with them.

Recognizing characteristics of the movement for a self-governing workshop within twentieth-century labor cultures has been obscured not only because of the presumption that it died out, but also because of the presence of socialists and syndicalists among labor organizers in Seattle and communist organizers in San Francisco. One of the first things that I noticed upon studying the Seattle and San Francisco general strikes was that the political orientations of labor organizers, and much of the rank and file, neither fit the class-consciousness mold nor exhibited the characteristics of "practical" AFL craft unionists. Although there were socialists and communists among labor activists, many of the "radicals" did not adhere to rigid ideologies and formulated doctrines or belong to political parties. Rather, the orientation of the labor factions that mobilized these general strikes is best described as pragmatic radicalism, exhibiting a resonance for specific narratives, strategies, and practices reminiscent of the movement for the self-governing workshop.

Yet the European model of class consciousness has contributed to the dismissal of the movement for a self-governing workshop as a source of narratives and practices for labor organizations within industrial societies, diverting our attention from the fact that they are embedded within American class identities to this day. There are at least three teleological presumptions, which write inevitable outcomes into history, that can be identified in the common usage of the term. First are the Marxist categories that define important class actors as either owners (the bourgeoisie) or wage workers (the proletariat). This definition precludes or demeans the importance of small landowners and artisans—those who at once labor, own, and control the means of production. Among the scholars who have recognized this problem is Charles Bergquist, who takes issue with capitalist/wage-worker categories when they are applied to Latin American conditions because they do not recognize the struggles of "rural laborers," "sharecroppers," and "small holders." He argues that most Marxists view such people as "petty capitalists" and have "neglected the fact that these same people also control the way they work and the products of their labor."[16]

A similar concern was expressed about small landowners in the United States. In *The Populist Moment: A Short History of the Agrarian Revolt in America*, historian Lawrence Goodwyn has stated that one of the obstacles to understanding the Populist movement is related to commonly used concepts of class. This classification of individuals as either owners or wage workers when "applied to the agrarian revolt in America, will merely succeed in rendering the Populist experience invisible." He continues: "While classes in agricultural societies contain various shadings of 'property consciousness' on the part of rich landowners, small holders, and landless laborers ('gentry,' 'farmers' and 'tenants,' in American terminology), these distinctions create more problems than they solve when applied to the agrarian revolt. It is a long-standing assumption . . . that 'landowners' must perforce behave in politically reactionary ways. The political aspirations of the landless are seen to deserve intense scrutiny, but the politics of 'the landed' cannot be expected to contain serious progressive ideas."[17]

The class-consciousness concept is also teleological in its presumption that industrial societies are inevitably progressing toward greater state centralization, requiring that problems of inequality be resolved through a Keynesian welfare state or by socialists who gain control of the state to reorganize the economy. Consequently, labor organizations that sought models of economic change in which the state was not the locus of redistribution, like the Knights' cooperatives for production and distribution, have been dismissed as "backward looking." Even when labor organized as industrial workers, as did the Industrial Workers of the World (IWW), their goals of union ownership and control of industries and their rejection of the state as the vehicle of change led to similar characterizations. Although states did become more centralized within twentieth-century industrial societies, they did not exhibit the same degree of centralization, nor were these trends irreversible, as the dissolution of the Soviet Union and the dismantling of the American welfare state has illustrated.

Finally, class consciousness implicitly assumes that there is something intrinsic to industrial economies that results in the failure of worker-owned and controlled industries. Much of the existing scholarly literature describes the Knights' cooperatives as failing because of their grounding in a "mythical" preindustrial past. In other words there was something about the process of industrialization that rendered this type of economic organization obsolete. This presumption neglects the many alliances of state actors with employers, resulting in a violent yet legal repression of labor. The Knights' cooperatives also failed for many of the same reasons that other industries failed in the late nineteenth century: competition, lack of funds or business experience, and the power of growing monopolies to withhold needed capital and transportation. The demise of labor-owned enterprises along with labor organizations does not support the assumption that the process of industrialization made worker-owned and controlled industries obsolete. The viability of cooperatives in other industrial nations indicates otherwise.

These teleological presumptions have "invalidated" models for an egalitarian political economy proposed by movements with the largest mass followings in U.S. history—the Knights and the Populist Party. Viewing American labor through a lens of class consciousness set up the political template for what are considered "realistic" paths to egalitarian social change within industrial and postindustrial societies. This in turn has limited the recognition of preindustrial narratives embedded within political cultures that provided justifications for mobilizing general strikes. Labor historian Bruce Laurie has rightly pointed out that the producerist radicalism of the Knights, which linked the right to wealth with the production of goods, although common during the early stages of industrialization in other nations, lasted longer in the United States than in any continental nation.[18]

Since the 1960s, the "new labor history" has examined the ways that artisans have drawn on preindustrial cultural understandings to protest labor disempowerment within industrial societies. While the connotations of agrarian "languages" were transformed with changing economic conditions, strands of these languages continued to resonate.[19] Moral and political philosophies from the early republic, foremost those of Jefferson and Paine, were drawn on and transformed, yet strands were retained through the artisan republican vocabularies of the labor movement for the self-governing workshop. But before we can identify these continuities within the political cultures in Seattle and San Francisco and analyze how the political cultures were instrumental during both general strikes, we must first look at the narratives and practices of Jefferson, Paine, and artisan republicanism through a different lens.

THE EARLY REPUBLIC'S CULTURE OF CONTRADICTIONS

The American revolutionaries elicit a multitude of responses, from sacred reverence to dismissal as hypocrites and elite landowners concerned only about property rights. I ask the reader to suspend judgment and consider the moral and political theories of Jefferson and Paine in a different light. Many people assume that the framers embraced neoliberal economic values that are dominant today. It is true that they believed in the right to private property and participated in liberal economic discourses associated with English philosopher John Locke. But these discourses were intertwined with the classical republican ones associated with the civic humanism of Renaissance thought as well as English republicanism.[20] The civic humanist strands embodied in classical republicanism carried on characterizations of human nature elaborated by Aristotle and other classical Greek as well as by Roman thinkers. From scholar Carl Boggs: "Aristotle wrote that human beings are by their very nature political creatures insofar as the sphere of political participation inevitably entails higher values—a life of public commitment, a sense of giving and selflessness, a passion for learning, growth and enlightenment."[21]

The framers supported the right to private property, promoted expanding markets, and most made money through land speculation. But if we define capitalism as a society in which the majority of the population sells labor power as a commodity, the early republic was not capitalist.[22] The political economy that the framers lived in was quite different from today, and it is important that we understand their narratives, particularly those of Jefferson and Paine, within their historical context. A closer look at the early republic reveals a society with markets, workplaces, and understandings of citizenship quite different from current characterizations.

At the time of the American Revolution the majority of the population labored in some form of agrarian production or were artisans (including some slaves) or small shopkeepers. Through territorial expansion, tax-subsidized military protection, and state contracts that enabled private property rights to exist, Euro-American male citizens secured land for minimal amounts—in some cases for only the cultivation of it. Unlike English tenant farmers most colonial farmers owned their own land.[23] For most of the population there was little separation between the workplace and home and only minor distinctions between employer and employee within craft workshops. The male artisan, or mechanic, both supplied capital and labored within the workplace in close association with journeymen, skilled workers who were paid wages, and apprentices (usually teenagers who received room and board as they learned the trade).

Colonial women were for the most part excluded from "male" trades. The majority of women engaged in agrarian home production, which included growing and preserving food; making candles, soap, and clothing; and acting as both doctors and midwives for their families. Some women, however, were innkeepers, ran sawmills and dry good stores, made furniture, and were often the town undertakers. When women were apprenticed, it was in spinning, weaving, and the skills of household production.[24]

Because most markets were local in the early republic and banks and impersonal forms of credit did not exist, exchanges were mediated as social and moral actions. It was said that "trade ought to be managed with truth, justice and charity: for without these . . . it is only a more cleanly act of cheating and oppression."[25] Through the early 1820s merchants in New York still paid journeymen apprentices a "just price," indicating that their wage labor was not yet considered a commodity subject to market demand and there was an assize on bread or municipal price control.[26] In fact, it was common for mechanics in the late eighteenth century to expect the state to stabilize the economy and stimulate growth.[27]

The public speeches of most revolutionaries exhibited agreement that a roughly equitable distribution of property among "citizens" was essential for a republican form of government (meaning a republic or representative democracy as opposed to a monarchy).[28] Property requirements to vote were in place to minimize the corrupting impact of economic dependence, which created power imbalances. Power was often conceptualized as a "cancer" that would spread to consume liberty if it were not constrained, because human beings easily became "intoxicated" with it. The only legitimate basis for the exercise of power was through the "mutual consent" of those subjected to it.[29] Property provided independence from coercion and minimized the likelihood of political prostitution. In the early republic there were rich and poor, but the distinction between them was minimal compared with Europe. For example, George Washington's estate was equivalent to a "better sort of yeoman" in England.[30]

Citizen ownership of property also provided the leisure time for personal and intellectual development that was essential to participation in a republic. As American Enlightenment thinkers, influenced by classical authors and the republics of Greece and Rome, the framers promoted "liberal education," history, languages, and philosophy as preparation for political participation. Jefferson argued that to safeguard the republic, the public must be educated; he supported funding public education along with libraries and art galleries.

Republicanism was a fluid political orientation, which meant different things to many different people. In rural communities the colonists constructed republicanism in moralistic terms as an attack on outside forces and hierarchy. Those living in regions where a market economy was expanding and wealth inequalities were emerging adopted republican narratives of equality and opportunity for all, while new merchants within urban areas were drawn to republicanism's challenge to aristocratic privileges and the idleness and lack of talent that went along with such privileges.[31]

Yet, as Laurie has pointed out, republicanism exhibited coherence through discourses that posed "an enduring tension between virtue and commerce, the self and the market."[32] Political officials were expected to develop "disinterestedness," defined as being "superior to regard of private advantage; not influenced by private profit."[33] More than other forms of government, republics depended on the morality and civic virtue of the citizenry. Those who were dependent on the market for wages or whose market pursuits were driven by the need for profits were therefore considered "unfit" for political office.[34]

Through books, journals, and congressional accounts from the early republic, the historian James L. Huston has identified two dominant narratives that explained how a roughly equitable distribution of wealth could be maintained. He writes: "First, equitability was achieved in wealth distribution when all citizens adhered to the labor theory of property/value. Second, distortions in the distribution of wealth arose primarily from politics—specifically, in the policies that aristocrats devised to transfer the fruits of others' labors to themselves."[35] From the early republic through the Civil War, the right to property was morally justified through "the labor theory of property/value." In other words anyone who didn't directly labor to produce goods or services had no right to the wealth created. All of the subsequent U.S. presidents after Jefferson and including Lincoln shared this belief, and it was a dominant narrative within the early republic.[36]

But for a republic of "citizens" with a roughly equitable distribution of wealth, a state was needed that would not produce "distortions in the distribution of wealth" or allow elites to "transfer the fruits of others' labors to themselves." The calls for laissez-faire were directed at monarchical states that engaged in patronage relationships which provided unfair advantages for the aristocracy. Laissez-faire policies were directed at minimizing state privileges that produced trade monopolies and economic and political oligarchies. The framers criticized excessive taxation because in Europe it was the mechanism for allowing the "nonproductive" aristocracy to appropriate the wealth created through the labor of colonists.

Such were the dominant narratives of the landed gentry, including most of the framers, during the early republic. Yet this concept of an egalitarian republic was built on a culture of contradictions from its inception. The framers' rhetoric of obtaining the fruits of one's labor and liberty through roughly equitable property ownership was in stark contrast to the practices of slavery, the patriarchal control of women, and the decimation of indigenous societies to expand territory for "citizens" to maintain independent livelihoods. The social contract of the early republic was at the same time a "racial contract" and a "sexual contract," or the tacit agreement among most "citizens" not to see such contradictions.[37]

The vision of an egalitarian republic initially applied to a small circle of people, and the framers' opinions differed on the question of who were fit to be "citizens." Within monarchies physical labor was demeaned and seen as necessary drudgery; those of lower economic and social status engaged in it. Despite the republican rhetoric of equality, however, most of the colonial gentry did not think that artisans, small landholders, and least of all slaves or Euro-American women were capable of rational political action. George Washington referred to small farmers and landholders as "the grazing multitude," while Pennsylvania representative Gouverneur Morris was concerned that the common people had "no morals but their own interests."[38]

Among the framers Jefferson's and Paine's political philosophies were the most egalitarian of the time. Jefferson himself was a member of the landed gentry and owned slaves. Paine came from an artisan's background, yet the political thoughts of each man overlapped in numerous areas.[39] When Paine's second part of *The Rights of Man*—which proposed state-funded popular education, pensions for the aged, and state employment for unemployed laborers—was attacked by conservatives, Jefferson defended Paine by stating that he himself deserved the same criticism because "I profess the same principles." Jefferson saw *The Rights of Man* as an "antidote to the 'political heresies' of the reactionary Federalists."[40]

Jefferson's often quoted statement that the "state that governs least, governs best" did not preclude a proactive role for the state in securing resources for "citizens." In a draft of the Virginia Constitution he proposed that every citizen in the state receive fifty acres of land. Returning to the epigraph at the opening of this chapter, in his *Agrarian Justice* Paine called for society to provide "fifteen pounds sterling" to all citizens, not as charity but as indemnification or payment for loss of their "natural inheritance" of the earth through the privatization of property. Paine went on to argue: "But the earth in its natural state, as before said, is capable of supporting but a small number of inhabitants compared with what it is capable of doing in a cultivated state. And it is impossible to separate the improvement made by cultivation from the earth itself, upon which that improvement is made, the idea of landed property arose from that inseparable connection; but it is nevertheless true, that it is the value of the improvement only, and not the earth itself, that is individual property. Every proprietor, therefore, of cultivated lands, owes to the community a *ground-rent* . . . for the land which he holds."[41]

Such proposals were understandable, given Jefferson's and Paine's belief that property in its natural state belonged to all people on earth and that private ownership resulted from state intervention late in human history. It was the cultivation of land or the labor put into it that guaranteed the right to use it. But the state and those who appropriated property through cultivation had an obligation to compensate people who had been dispossessed of their "natural inheritance." Jefferson articulated ideas similar to Paine's in a 1785 letter to James Madison: "The earth is given as a common stock for man [*sic*] to labor and live on. If for the encouragement of industry we allow it to be appropriated, we must take care that other employment be provided to those excluded from the appropriation. *If we do not, the fundamental right to labor the earth returns to the unemployed.* . . . It is not too soon to provide by every possible means that as few as possible shall be without a little portion of land."[42]

Jefferson's point that the right to land returns to the unemployed if society does not provide employment for them has been overlooked for far too long. Although recognizing the impossibility of absolutely equal property distribution, Jefferson affirmed the role of the state in his 1785 letter to Madison to safeguard as wide a distribution as possible: "[The] unequal division of property . . . occasions the numberless instances of wretchedness which . . . is to be observed all over Europe. . . . I am conscious that an equal division of property is impracticable. But [given] the consequences of this enormous inequality producing so much misery to the bulk of mankind, legislators cannot invent too many devices for subdividing property."[43] To further secure "citizen" access to resources, Virginia had laws against charging interest above 5 percent "for the loan of moneys," a point made by Jefferson when writing to French aristocrat Marquis de Barbé-Marbois.[44]

Given his moral and political philosophy, Jefferson perhaps best epitomized the culture of contradictions. He was a slave owner, yet in the Declaration of Independence he wrote an excoriating attack on the British slave trade, which was deleted from the Declaration's final version.[45] One of Jefferson's first acts as governor of Virginia in 1774 was to propose a law that allowed "owners" to set slaves free; it did not pass, however. The law eventually did change, but Jefferson never set his slaves free. Jefferson had racist views toward African Americans, yet he hoped that the malleability of human nature would prove him wrong. He was convinced that emancipation was inevitable. Indicative of how the subordination of women was deeply embedded within his culture, Jefferson presumed that women's dependent position was "natural" and he could not conceptualize this form of stratification in terms of power relations or exploitation. But he believed that male small freeholders and artisans were capable of political participation in a republic.

Differentiating themselves from the elite gentry, artisans saw their labor as the "very embodiment of republican values" and the essence of an egalitarian republic. Their identities were transformed dramatically through the revolutionary experience as they joined forces with the gentry to fight for independence. Artisans were among the first to respond to Paine's *Common Sense* by pressuring committees of merchants and professionals to take more radical action.[46] Artisan republicanism adopted dominant narratives within the early republic, especially the more egalitarian political theories of Jefferson and Paine, but they combined these theories with the principles of their trade cultures. As historian Howard B. Rock wrote: "Jeffersonian republicans seized upon this new identity and drew these mechanics into their political orbit in the 1790s by recognizing the artisan's role as part of an independent producing class, ensuring Thomas Jefferson's election to the presidency in 1800."[47]

As the circle of inclusion within the new republic widened to include Euro-American male artisans by the early nineteenth century, other divisions nurtured through the culture of contradictions remained well entrenched within American institutions and culture. These divisions would create barriers to solidarity among exploited and disempowered groups as the process of capitalist industrialization changed citizen-owners into wage workers. Building on artisan republican traditions, the labor movement for the self-governing workshop would eventually challenge this culture of contradictions.

Through the process of capitalist industrialization in the nineteenth century the livelihoods of artisans and small landholders changed dramatically. The local markets, often based on a system of barter and exchange, were replaced with national markets that were oriented toward the accumulation of profit. Opportunities for trade increased after the revolution, and western migrants created new markets. Within the agrarian economy of the early republic, there existed "built-in" ceilings on how much wealth could be produced.[48] Improvements in machinery and communication provided an opportunity for the accumulation of wealth by merchants in ways that had not formerly existed. Some masters and small merchants became manufacturers for larger markets. Specialization, which relied on laborers with less skill, reduced the cost of labor and increased productivity and profits.

Not all employers embraced the idea of breaking down the labor process to produce at less cost, however. The cultural transition to market reductionism or "pecuniary values," where gaining profit became the ruling logic, was a slow one.[49] In 1830 an aspiring merchant from England, John Petheram, found this out in New York. Upon noticing the "apparent backwardness" of employers who did not realize that dividing labor could produce more products, he suggested the idea to several small shopkeepers. The angry response of drug maker John Morrison was typical: "This, Sir, is a free country. . . . We want no one person over another, which would be the case if you divided the labor." Another shopkeeper told Petheram: "Tories may be very well in England but we want none here."[50]

Although skilled craftsmen were still the majority in the early nineteenth century, as their traditional livelihoods were threatened by new forms of less skilled production, craft-based mutual aid societies were transformed into trade unions. Aside from isolated strikes by Philadelphia shoemakers in 1792 and New York printers in 1794, the first movement of wage laborers in the United States emerged in the 1830s.[51] The concept of the strike, through which workers withhold their labor power, became prevalent with the growing divide between employers and wage laborers through the process of capitalist industrialization.[52] Within the changing economy of the nineteenth century, a minority of the master craftsmen became entrepreneurs while other mechanics and journey-men found intermediary positions between manual labor and the emerging middle class of manufacturers and bankers. A third group lost livelihoods and skills, however, and fell into manual wage labor.[53] Some wage workers and artisans who lost their livelihoods moved West to obtain cheap land.

Yet the culture of contradictions was also expressed through the pro-ducerist narratives that claimed new territories for Euro-American male "citizens." The right to property through the cultivation of it justified the dispossession of indigenous populations. As historian David Roedi-ger has written: "Settler ideology held that improvident, sexually aban-doned 'lazy Indians' were failing to 'husband' or 'subdue' the resources God had provided and thus should forfeit those resources. Work and whiteness joined in the argument for dispossession."[54] The "Indian" was admired by some, including Jefferson, as independent and creative in contrast with the servility of slaves and free blacks.

Roediger has argued that working-class formation in the nineteenth century was related to "whiteness" (and masculinity) because it was con-structed in contrast to slavery.[55] He insightfully points out that in no other nation has chattel slavery been present during the years in which the industrial working class was born. The Enlightenment discourses of lib-erty, progress, and manifest destiny were used to justify slavery and to subjugate indigenous populations and women.[56] Yet the tensions within Enlightenment discourses of reason, equality, and freedom with prac-tices of exploitation and subjugation generated movements that chal-lenged these contradictions, including ones among Euro-American male "citizens" who were being dispossessed of their property and liveli-hoods through capitalist industrialization.

As small producers and journeymen attempted to thwart workplace disempowerment, they "turned to the language of the republic to explain their views" through their own "democratic variant of American repub-lican ideology."[57] At this time we see the beginnings of the movement for the self-governing workshop. By the 1820s and 1830s numerous writ-ings addressing the changing circumstances of the economy were cir-culating. Among them were the proposals of radical artisans Langton Byllesby and Thomas Skidmore.

Byllesby was a printer by trade who venerated Jefferson, but his pro-posals for mitigating social problems, while congruent with Jeffersonian principles, moved beyond them. He argued that life, liberty, and the pursuit of happiness could not be secured within an unequal economy. He proposed creating a society of cooperative production where "artisans would invest a sum to pay for all materials and would themselves be paid in labor notes, in proportion to the amount of work they actually performed." He condemned the emerging system of manipulated credit and capitalist exploitation as "unrepublican denials of 'true liberty and just government.'"[58] Skidmore was a New York artisan influenced by Paine and the radical British economists known as the Ricardians. Drawing on the labor theory of property/value, he called for a constitutional convention that would "void all titles and debts, provide for a survey of real and personal property and then redistribute proportional shares to each man when he reached the age of twenty-one."[59] The use of the term "man" was generic, as Skidmore also supported women's rights.

Many artisans losing their livelihoods, subsistence farmers, and Southern planters became Jacksonian Democrats. They appropriated the legacy of Jefferson and emphasized civic virtue, maintaining workplace control, individualism, but foremost equality. The Jacksonians represented one variant of free labor ideology, which drew on artisan republican and radical republican vocabularies and sought to maintain widely distributed property through which worker-owners received the fruits of their labor. This variant of free labor ideology adamantly opposed monopolies of wealth and power that threatened the livelihoods of small producers and artisans. In the name of laissez-faire they challenged corporate charters and state subsidies to businesses, which provided an unfair legal advantage to industrial capitalists and financiers. These Jacksonians saw themselves as keeping watch over the "charter mongers and money changers out to use the state for personal advantage" and called for "equal rights for all, and special privileges for none."[60] Other Jacksonians called for the abolition of hereditary wealth, which interfered with the "free trade" of each generation.

Yet Jacksonian Democrats participated in the culture of contradictions, supporting the myth of manifest destiny and placing the national unity above the abolition of slavery. Some of them would eventually join the Republican Party of Lincoln. In addition to their differentiation from slaves, wage laborers in the Jacksonian era had their rights established through vocabularies that equated "manhood" with independence and control. Thus figuratively masculinized, the artisan republican values of independence made it difficult for males to recognize common interests with emerging female semiskilled factory workers.[61]

Ascendant merchant capitalists adopted another variant of free labor ideology. They also drew on the labor theory of property/value and republican vocabularies to legitimate their rights to private property and to wealth created in the workplace. They also envisioned a society with wide access to property, through which all could receive the fruits of their labor. But merchant capitalists argued that opportunity existed for those who were industrious, and they increasingly drew on the ideas of economist Adam Smith to justify a market economy directed by the laws of supply and demand.[62] This group of merchants found themselves at odds with the ascendant movement for the self-governing workshop. Eventually, leading manufacturers would draw less on the shared idiom of free labor ideology to justify their rights through Social Darwinism.[63]

The cooperative movements of the 1840s and 1850s appropriated some of the narratives and strategies of the Jacksonians while constructing new ones. With the growing concentration of landownership, laborers looked to middle-class land reformers and cooperative movements as solutions to "wage slavery" in light of the changing scale and organization of the economic system.[64] It was common for middle-class reformers to attend labor organization meetings. For example, in 1844 the New England Working Men's Association meeting was attended by Horace Greeley, Robert Owen, and George Henry Evans. Evans sought national labor support for his land reform proposals. Drawing on the early republic's vision of equality through widespread ownership of land, he proposed to end land monopolies, to decrease the concentration of ownership through laws that limited the amount of land that any individual could own, and to distribute freely public lands to settlers.[65]

The NLU continued to draw on artisan republican discursive strands into the 1860s. The NLU's producerist narratives argued for a roughly equitable distribution of land to sustain a democracy. In the platform written at their 1868 convention, they affirmed that:

We hold these truths to be self-evident: that all people are created equal. . . . We further hold that property or wealth is the product of physical or intellectual labor employed in the productive industry, and in the distributions of productive labor that laborers ought of right, and would, under a just monetary system, receive or retain the larger proportions of their productions;

that the wrongs, oppressions and destitutions which laborers are suffering in most departments of legitimate enterprise and useful occupation do not result from insufficiency of production, but from the unfair distribution of the products of labor between non-producing capital and labor . . .

We further hold that it is essential to the happiness and prosperity of the people and the stability of our democratic-republican institutions that the public domain be distributed as widely as possible among the people, a land monopoly being equally as oppressive to the people and as dangerous to our institutions as the present money monopoly. To prevent this, the public lands should be given in reasonable quantities, and to none but actual occupants.[66]

The NLU's platform epitomizes the concerns of the movement for the self-governing workshop that there had been a rupture between labor and access to the wealth produced by it through the concentration of land and wealth in the hands of nonproductive merchant capitalists.

To enhance labor strength and solidarity in light of growing numbers of less skilled wage workers, the NLU confronted the culture of contradictions by opening the union to women and people of color, although inclusion was minimally practiced. The NLU was shortlived, but in its wake came the Knights of Labor. The Knights wanted to have public ownership of a few public-interest industries to undermine monopoly control, but their vision of an egalitarian society was one in which ownership and control of industries stayed in the hands of those who worked in them.

Recognizing that an economy of small landowners was no longer possible, the Knights pursued a transformed economy that would maintain the principles of Jefferson and Paine within an industrialized society. They sought to abolish the wage system and replace it with an industrial system of large-scale cooperatives for production and distribution. They challenged the concentration of wealth and power and "unjust accumulation," which was hurting the producing classes, those who labored directly in the workplace, rather than nonproductive capitalists, absentee owners, and stockholders. The Knights "grew out of the reform and humanitarian movements of ante-bellum America, and was the direct descendant . . . of the labor reform tradition of the Jacksonian Era."[67] Labor autonomy for the Knights included the organization of labor courts to try both workplace and civil violations of workers.[68] They continued the NLU's challenge to the culture of contradictions through inclusive unionism. The practice of inclusion varied by region, yet the Knights did succeed in establishing a national membership that was roughly one-tenth women and one-tenth African American.[69]

The Knights organized numerous cooperatives that failed, partly because of the growing power of monopolies. One example occurred when the coal miners at Cannelberg, Indiana, asked the Knights for help after the Buckeye Coal Company had forced them into unemployment. The Knights leased an adjoining property, "sunk a shaft and equipped it," and organized it as a cooperative. But when the coal was ready to ship, the Ohio and Mississippi Railway Company failed to lay a switch to the mine, which they had agreed to do. It was discovered that directors of the Railway Company also owned the Buckeye mine, which competed with the new miners' cooperative.[70]

The Knights went into decline by the 1890s due to conflicts with railroad tycoons, lost strikes, state repression, and internal organizational problems. The movement for the self-governing workshop, however, did not die out with them. By the Seattle general strike in 1919, a political culture existed that exhibited some narratives and practices of the movements for a self-governing workshop. New practices and narratives were also being constructed. This political culture retained the artisan republican vision of a republic of labor but adapted it to the economic and political conditions of the early twentieth century. What did this political culture look like in the twentieth century? What narratives, strategies, and practices mobilized workers to participate in general strikes in Seattle in 1919 and San Francisco in 1934?

POLITICAL CULTURES OF WORKPLACE DEMOCRACY

Political culture is a useful concept for understanding how labor factions were mobilized in these cases.[71] Political cultures are constituted by numerous orientations toward political action that often share ethical beliefs about just distributions of resources and power and the rights and obligations people have to each other. Yet within regions and occupational communities some political orientations, strategies, and practices are part of local histories and hence are familiar to social actors whether they agree with them or not. Dominant political narratives are among the conceptual frames through which participants of political cultures look at the world, including those who disagree but are forced to respond to these prevalent conceptual frames.

Specific types of political cultures become dominant because of the histories of political and economic struggles within those specific regions and the resources that people had to construct, communicate, and sustain them. Political culture, like all culture, is shared and therefore is both external and material. We can identify culture most easily if we think of it as consisting of "signs"—that is, anything produced by human beings that communicates meaning to others, be it language, text, sounds, gestures, body positions, eye contact, practices, and the organization of space or artifacts, from clothing to buildings. All of these cultural signs are material. They can be seen, felt, heard; people who share cultures communicate with each other through such signs.[72] In other words culture is material and like any other human production is contingent on the resources through which it is produced and the technologies, including modes of transportation, through which it is communicated.

A specific type of political culture became part of regional histories in Seattle and at West Coast ports as it diffused through occupational networks within these geographical regions. The Knights were active in the Seattle region in the nineteenth century, as were socialists and the IWW. (Organizational links between the Knights and the IWW are discussed more fully in chapter two.) Scholars have documented the early-twentieth-century occupational interchange among Pacific Northwest loggers, many of whom had been involved with the IWW, with longshoremen and sailors at West Coast ports. Through this regional and occupational interchange political cultures with some characteristics of the nineteenth-century self-governing workshop were exhibited among labor in Seattle in 1919 and in San Francisco in 1934. I call these twentieth-century clusters of interpretive frameworks and strategic repertoires "workplace democracy" political cultures. The term "workplace democracy" is intended to highlight the link of twentieth-century labor cultures with the nineteenth-century movement for the self-governing workshop. Labor analysts have called these political cultures and similar ones many names, including movements for "workers' control," "economic democracy," and "industrial democracy."[73] They have with some exceptions been analyzed mostly through class-consciousness lenses.

In both Seattle and San Francisco the workplace-democracy labor factions set the general strikes into motion. They successfully mobilized the rank and file through constructing appeals and practices resonant with the vision of the self-governing workshop, similar to using a "cultural tool kit."[74] Workplace-democracy political cultures are "ideal types" or analytical models, which are derived from political orientations in these cases.[75] Moderate, socialist, communist, and workplace-democracy labor factions may have acted differently in other times and places, but the narratives, strategies, and modes of organization described in this chapter best typify the political orientations in Seattle in 1919 and San Francisco in 1934. These ideal types simplify complex realities and political orientations that were fluid and intermeshed. Yet there is a cluster of characteristics differentiating workplace-democracy political orientations that can be identified.

The most distinguishing characteristic of workplace-democracy culture, and discursive strands most reminiscent of the movement for the self-governing workshop, was the promotion of worker ownership and management of industries. Like the Knights, Seattle unionists sought to "abolish the wage system" through a variety of strategies. Numerous worker cooperatives and labor-owned businesses were established for production and distribution, including the first daily labor newspaper, a theater, various types of stores, and a savings and loan as well as the promotion of "union label" consumption. In their 1919 longshoremen strike Seattle labor requested wage increases along with a share of ownership, profits, and directorates of the employing companies.[76] A radio address by longshoremen during the 1934 San Francisco general strike communicated the narrative of worker control by stating that "it is the intrinsic right as well as the acquired right of every American worker to organize and control the job."[77] One of the two central issues, which the International Longshoremen's Association (ILA) refused to arbitrate, was a union-controlled hiring hall.

The workplace-democracy emphasis on worker control and worker ownership of the industries was distinct from moderate trade unionism, which sought only "a fair day's wage for a fair day's work" and better working conditions. It also differed from the reform socialists, who proposed public ownership of industries through the state, or the communists, who saw the need for a socialist stage of state redistribution of resources prior to the emergence of communism. A second distinguishing characteristic of this political culture was the emphasis on participatory democracy and the rejection of centralized authority—be it bureaucratic officials within unions, unions within federations, or citizens within the state.

Organizers promoted rank-and-file control within unions. The rank and file approved policies through referendums rather than accepting the decisions of bureaucratic AFL officials or the directives of Communist Party (CP) leadership. Union autonomy within the federation was also prioritized in both political cultures: without it rank-and-file control was rendered meaningless. Some workplace democracyists promoted public ownership of a few industries that would be managed by the workers themselves. The key to the acceptance of public ownership of industries was worker management and local control of them. Other activists rejected the state entirely in favor of direct action and the general strike as the means through which control of industries would be directly transferred to those who labored in them.[78] In contrast, the reform socialists and communists promoted state ownership of the means of production, although the reform socialists emphasized worker management of industries. They also supported rank-and-file control within unions, but the goal of the CP was to gain control of the unions with a centralized party leadership deciding policies.

Workplace-democracy political culture was also characterized by a commitment to social issues that went far beyond bread-and-butter concerns. Workplace democracyists recognized the interconnections among economic, political, and social problems. In Seattle the labor-owned *Seattle Union Record* editorialized on a range of national and international political issues. The Seattle Central Labor Council (SCLC) took stands on political issues that did not directly concern union policies. An example of this was their public opposition to World War I. Seattle longshoremen refused to load munitions destined for General Aleksandr Kolchak's counterrevolutionary forces in Russia. The longshoremen at the San Francisco port distinguished themselves among American unions through their political actions. In the 1930s they refused to load shipments to Japan after the Japanese invasion of China or to Italy after Mussolini invaded Ethiopia. The longshoremen began the practice of racial inclusion at the San Francisco port during the 1934 coastwide strike, and the union spoke out against Japanese internment in the United States during World War II.[79]

Workplace-democracy organizers can also be identified through their promotion of inclusive industrial unionism of all members within industries, regardless of skill, race, nationality, or gender.[80] They sought to organize on a class, not craft, basis, as did the moderate AFL unions. Many of Seattle's unions had industrial contracts, and the SCLC representatives regularly promoted industrial organization at national AFL conferences. During the coastwide maritime strike the second point the longshoremen refused to negotiate, equal in importance to a worker-controlled hiring hall, was a coastwide contract of all West Coast ports. CP labor organizers also emphasized the importance of inclusive unions after massive post–World War I strike loss related to strikebreakers of color. Yet reform (as opposed to revolutionary) socialists rarely promoted racial inclusion in practice, even though their narratives emphasized racial equality.

Workplace-democracy cultures exhibited a rhetoric of class conflict. However, class was broadly defined as all laborers who directly produced goods and services as opposed to those who didn't. The term "capitalist," loosely used, applied to those who did not produce goods and services but appropriated wealth. The concept of "producer class" best fits the narrative, especially in the Seattle case, as opposed to "nonproductive capitalists" and absentee employers. The ethic that labor creates wealth and has a right to the wealth they produced was central to Seattle labor's narratives of injustice. Longshoremen mobilization appeals in San Francisco consistently emphasized that they did the "real work," but exploitative employers or "slave drivers" and union "buro-crats" got all the money produced through their labor. These distinctions in "ideal type" political orientations are summarized in Table 1.

To identify the workplace-democracy lineage and distinguish it from other political orientations, it is necessary to look for the *combination of characteristics* within a labor faction's mobilization appeals and practices. Resonant workplace-democracy narratives and practices were both similar to and different from other ideal type political orientations and have often been conflated with them. The narratives that "labor creates wealth" or the desire to "abolish the wage system," which were deeply embedded within artisan republican traditions, have too often been viewed through a class-consciousness lens and attributed to Marxism or other "foreign" ideologies.

Understanding political culture as constituting a resonance for certain narratives, strategies, and modes of organization helps us to move away from conceptualizing political orientations as rigid ideologies, doctrinaire formulas, or party policies that workers "followed." Many of the self-proclaimed radicals in these cases were not affiliated with nor did they take orders from any political organization. Recognizing the reso-

TABLE 1.

Ideal Type Political Orientations, Seattle (1919) and San Francisco (1934)

	Workplace Democracy	Moderate AFL	Reform Socialist	Communist
Worker ownership and/or management of industries	Yes	No	No/Yes	No
Anticentralized control:				
Union	Yes	No	Yes	Yes/No
Federation	Yes	No	Yes	Yes
State	Yes	Yes	No	No
Union commitment to social issues	Yes	No	Yes	Yes
Union inclusion	Yes	No	No	Yes
Rhetoric of class conflict	Yes	No	Yes	Yes

Sources: Newspapers, newsletters, meeting minutes, strike bulletins, flyers, oral histories, espionage reports, interviews, and letters from the Manuscripts & Archives Division and Special Collections at the University of Washington Libraries, Seattle; the ILWU Library, San Francisco; and the Bancroft Library, University of California–Berkeley.

nance among American workers for narratives and practices reminiscent of the labor movement for the self-governing workshop is essential to rethinking the American exceptionalism debate. American labor did seek to transform capitalist relations, but these models of social change have been obscured or dismissed through the lens of class consciousness.

OVERVIEW AND METHODS

This chapter has identified a type of political culture—workplace democracy—that exhibited discursive strands and practices from the nineteenth-century labor movement for the self-governing workshop during the Seattle and San Francisco general strikes. I have argued that identifying this political culture can help us to rethink the nature of American labor radicalism and its impact during collective action. The rest of the book answers my research questions: What conditions elicited these great strikes, and how were they justified by the participants? Was political culture, whether conservative or class-conscious, important at all?

Holistic case studies of the emergence, dynamics, and outcomes of each general strike (chapter 2 explores the Seattle strike while chapter 3 examines the San Francisco strike) describe the historical conditions out of which these great strikes emerged and how the participants justified the use of this tactic. These two chapters provide the information for a comparative analysis to follow in chapter four. First they present the history needed to make sense of these general strikes. Next these chapters explain how workplace-democracy political culture was present in Seattle and other West Coast ports to be used as a resource for labor organizers; they also examine its links to the labor movement for the self-governing workshop. Finally, chapters two and three identify how narratives, strategies, and practices were distinctive among workplace-democracy labor factions in contrast to moderate AFL craft unionists, reform socialists, and CP members.

The analytic logic of contrasting the political orientations of labor factions is to demonstrate how workers in similar occupational structures proposed different narratives, strategies, and practices with differing trajectories for action and outcomes. In other words, culture cannot be reduced to the logic of the organization of production. Given the opportunities and constraints within the same organization of production, political orientations of labor factions mediated the understanding of goals and strategies and what was and was not a resource. Political culture had an autonomous impact. I do not try to write new interpretations of two of the most studied general strikes in American history in these chapters; rather, I present the histories in a different way in which culture plays a salient role.

In chapter four a comparative analysis of the case studies identifies the ways that political culture was instrumental to the emergence, dynamics, and outcomes of both general strikes, especially to success in the San Francisco case. Returning to the different orientations of the labor factions, I assess the likelihood of a general strike having emerged had there been no workplace-democracy factions in either case. The comparative method of difference is then used to explain the differing dynamics and outcomes of the two general strikes.[81] This is accomplished through analyzing the cultural foundation for the generation of resources crucial to success in the San Francisco case. I also examine the relationship of resources to the flourishing, demise, and institutionalization of political cultures in both cases.

Chapter five builds on the insights that can be gained from recognizing the autonomous impact of culture in this book. I propose several arguments for consideration. First, these case studies indicate that effective labor mobilization challenging neoliberalism requires an alternative worldview derived through culturally embedded narratives that provide moral certitude and resonate with workers' identities. Second, many Americans did exhibit antistate orientations different from the European or class-conscious model; these were historically formed through the organization of the state, a legal system that privileged private property, and easy access to land. Third, among other twentieth-century developments the changing meaning of socialism since the post-Lenin era has contributed to the distancing of American labor from the left. I conclude the book by suggesting that we rethink routes to economic and political equality in the twenty-first century by drawing on resonant narratives of Jefferson, Paine, and artisan republicanism in innovative ways.

2 "A NEW POWER AND A NEW WORLD"

The Seattle General Strike, 1919

What scares them most is that NOTHING HAPPENS! They are ready for
DISTURBANCES. They have machine guns and soldiers, but this SMILING
SILENCE is uncanny. The businessmen don't understand this kind of
weapon. It comes from a different world than they live in. Yet most of them
might be real pleasant HUMAN BEINGS except that life has separated
them too much from common folks. It is the system of industry that
makes them sullen and SUSPICIOUS of us, not any natural depravity.
It is the system that trains them to believe that they can bring in enough
armed force to operate our industries. But how many MACHINE GUNS
will it take to cook ONE MEAL? It is your SMILE that is UPSETTING their
reliance on ARTILLERY. . . . It is the garbage wagons that go along the
street marked "EXEMPT by STRIKE COMMITTEE." It is the milk stations
that are getting better daily. And the three hundred WAR veterans of
Labor handling the crowds WITHOUT GUNS. For these things speak of
a NEW POWER and a NEW WORLD that they do not feel at HOME in.

—*History Committee of the General Strike Committee, 1919*

T he Seattle general strike occurred during a time of immense economic and political change both nationally and internationally.
For a short period after World War I, anything seemed possible.
The first "workers state" in human history, the Soviet Union (referring
to a union of workers councils called "soviets"), had been established
through revolution just two years earlier. At this historical moment Seattle labor exhibited perhaps the most vibrant workplace-democracy cul-

ture in the United States, which is not surprising given the city's history. The process of industrialization in Seattle had taken place within a few decades, as did the transition from self-governing workshop vocabularies in the late nineteenth century to workplace-democracy narratives and practices among a unionized workforce in the twentieth.

This chapter looks closely at the economic, political, and historically contingent conditions out of which this general strike emerged. It also highlights the distinctive cultural lenses that mediated the strategies of workplace-democracy labor factions in contrast to moderate American Federation of Labor (AFL) unionists and reform socialists. This enables us to identify the different trajectories for action each group proposed and lays the groundwork to assess cultural impact in chapter four. The story begins with a discussion of organizations representative of the movement for the self-governing workshop in the Seattle area in the late nineteenth century. I look at how activists and organizations communicated strategies over time. Next I examine the economic and political changes that occurred during World War I and the flourishing of a vital workplace-democracy political culture, which set the stage for collective action. Finally, I focus on the precipitating metal trades strike and the general strike with a description of how the events unfolded. A discussion of post-strike developments concludes the chapter.

THE SELF-GOVERNING WORKSHOP IN SEATTLE HISTORY

Human beings make sense of their worlds through worldviews constructed from cultural material accessible from their social locations. To understand the resonance of workplace democracy narratives, strategies, and modes of organization among labor during Seattle's general strike, we must briefly review this region's history. Because of its history, geography, and occupational structure, the city had greater cultural resources than other regions through which to construct resonant appeals for workplace democracy.

Although the western United States industrialized later than the eastern part did, by the 1870s and 1880s Seattle had a fairly developed economy, with coal production, furniture manufacture, bakeries, breweries, retail stores, law offices, and banks through which services and products were purchased by residents and surrounding farming communities, mining outposts, and logging towns.[1] In the 1870s the Knights of Labor (hereafter the Knights) were active in Seattle. Drawing on artisanal republican themes, the Knights' goal was to maintain labor sovereignty over the production process through reorganization of the industrial workplace. They sought to create a nationwide system of industrial cooperatives for production and distribution managed by worker-owners. Such an economy could eliminate the "nonproductive" capitalists and "middlemen," who disproportionately appropriated the wealth created by labor. The Knights sought sovereignty over their own affairs and organized their own court system on the local and district levels to oversee violations of labor practices and civil law.[2]

Realizing that the strength of labor was dependent on solidarity across crafts and industries, the Knights attempted to be inclusive of race, gender, and the unskilled—but with mixed results. The legacy of contradictions—the early republic's promise of equality and liberty combined with its practices of exploitation and exclusion—continued to haunt the movement for the self-governing workshop. While admitting some women and African Americans, the Knights opposed the importation of lower-paid Chinese workers for the construction of the Great Northern Railroad in the 1880s and helped to organize anti-Chinese campaigns in Seattle.[3] Granted, many of the Chinese were "sojourners" who planned on returning to their countries and were not interested in joining unions. Yet many were not, and the degree of virulent racism expressed went way beyond legitimate concerns about wage depression.

Although the Knights were active in Seattle by the 1870s, the first central trade union to emerge was the Western Central Labor Union (WCLU) in 1888. It was politically moderate and concerned mostly with bread-and-butter wage issues typical of the ascendant AFL. Yet membership in the Knights continued to grow rapidly in Tacoma and Seattle after 1885. In a time when there were few free libraries, the Knights provided reading rooms in Seattle, Tacoma, and Spokane.[4]

In addition to the cultural impact of the Knights in Seattle, the Populist Party was active in the state of Washington. In 1898 the WCLU joined with others to form the Washington State Labor Congress, the primary goal of which was to promote the enactment of the Populist Party platform, which included prolabor reforms. Like other producers, farmers were being dispossessed of their livelihoods. The Knights and the Populists exhibited workplace-democracy characteristics, although the Populists had a predominantly agrarian base through the Farmers Alliances.

They envisioned a society for the "plain people," which would consist of farmer-owned cooperatives for production and distribution.[5] The Populist movement engaged in more coalitions with labor organizations in the West than in other regions.

Communitarian settlements added to the geographical concentration of organizations for a self-governing workshop in the Seattle region. In 1896 a group calling themselves the True Populists attempted to practically apply their "socialist" principles. The new organization, called the Brotherhood of the Cooperative Commonwealth (BCC), vowed to concentrate colonies and industries in one state until it became socialist. In 1887 the BCC's organizer, Eugene Debs, proposed a migration of socialists to some Western states. As Washington already had numerous communitarian settlements, the BCC vowed to make Washington the first socialist state in America.[6] The migration attracted urban and rural workers from the East. As a result of the migration a socialist press emerged. A number of Seattle general strike participants had been participants in or admirers of the BCC.

In Seattle, reform socialism exhibited some vocabularies and practices of the self-governing workshop. But to understand how proponents of state ownership of industries contributed to inclinations toward the self-governing workshop, it is first necessary to clarify what Debsian "socialism" meant to its adherents. In 1912, Debs won 6 percent of the presidential vote on the Socialist ticket. His industrial socialism emphasized control over the industries by those who worked in them. Debs stated that the union's purpose was to educate "the workers in the management of industrial activities . . . fitting them for cooperative control and democratic regulation of their trades."[7]

This was not the same as the current socialist model of centralized state control. Debsian socialism, which drew on both Marxism and cooperativist traditions, was the most resonant form of socialism among the American public. Debs's Socialist Party of America "absorbed elements not in harmony with its official Marxian character, elements drawn from the Georgist, Nationalist, cooperationist and communitarian past. Although officially Debsian socialism was a secular and 'scientific' movement to place the economy under government control, it had a strong millenarian and anti-government cast; although it was inherently hostile to communitarianism, it attracted a significant number of people who viewed socialism as a new basis on which they could actively organize their social lives for their own special benefit. For such people a vote for socialism was not a vote for the Socialist State but for an entirely new political order favorable to cooperative brotherhood."[8]

Other forms of socialism also resembled the movement for a self-governing workshop. For example, Lassallean socialism, promoted by some German immigrants, envisioned a society that "would establish cooperative factories and workshops subsidized by the government but owned and operated by workers."[9] These popular understandings of socialism were different from those that emerged in the post-Lenin era of socialism as state-centralized command economies, a point I discuss in more detail in chapter five.

By the late nineteenth century, Seattle labor participated in narratives, practices, and modes of organization reminiscent of cooperativism, the Knights, Debsian reform socialism, and moderate AFL craft unionism. Because of strike and membership losses, the Knights went into decline in Seattle by the 1890s. In 1902 the Western Central Labor Union affiliated with the national AFL and became the Seattle Central Labor Council (SCLC), which would organize the future general strike. Regional principles of workplace democracy were apparent as each local sent three workers as representatives to the SCLC, which the AFL did not require. Seattle unionists claimed that their locals had the highest participation rates in the country.[10]

The demise by the turn of the century of organizations supporting the self-governing workshop could have resulted in the dominance of moderate AFL craft unionism, but radical industrial unions established a foothold in what were to become two key industries in Washington—lumber and mining. These industries were organized from the beginning by the American Labor Union (ALU), an offshoot of the Western Federation of Miners (WFM). Many WFM members had formerly been in the Knights and brought both producerist narratives and inclusive strategies with them. The WFM welcomed "every class of toil, from the farmer to the skilled mechanic, in one great brotherhood."[11]

There were direct links among the Knights, the WFM, the ALU, and the IWW. After the Knights dissolved in Seattle by the turn of the century, the WFM became populated with "thousands" of former Knights.[12] WFM leader Bill Haywood and the ALU's Clarence Smith were among key organizers of the IWW in Chicago in 1905.[13] Through these links, and other forms of organizational and activist diffusion, discursive strands from the self-governing workshop continued through the IWW's vision of "industrial democracy" that would be established through rank-and-file control of the union and union control of industries.

The IWW is often described as having "syndicalist" political orientations; its first manifesto, according to one of its authors, was based on the organization of labor in continental Europe—meaning revolutionary syndicalism.[14] The IWW also exhibited some narratives and practices similar to European syndicalism, specifically the rejection of a centralized state and reliance on trade unions and the general strike (instead of political parties) to create a worker-controlled economy. Georges Sorel was the most famous revolutionary syndicalist. His book *Reflections on Violence* was widely circulated in Europe and the United States in the first two decades of the twentieth century. He argued that a "militant minority," not so different from Lenin's vanguard party, was needed to make revolution. Through their attacks on rationality and bourgeois moralism, revolutionary syndicalists justified the use of violence to accomplish their ends.

But the rejection of a centralized state and preference for worker-controlled industries were also characteristics of the movement for the self-governing workshop, which predated revolutionary syndicalism. There were important differences. Although some American syndicalists, like William Foster, adopted the militant minority rhetoric, and some references could be found in IWW literature, most IWW members were hyperdemocratic in practice.[15] They believed in unions controlled by the rank and file and that any member could be an organizer. Another important distinction was the IWW's outreach to unskilled workers within industries, which was not common to French syndicalism.[16] The IWW's industrial unionism inclusive of race, nationality, and gender was more similar to the Knights, whose motto was "An injury to one is the concern of all." The IWW's motto was "An injury to one is an injury to all." Also different was the IWW's interpretation of "sabotage," which to most members meant slowing down the work process but not harming people. Nevertheless opponents used the term "sabotage" to compare the IWW with European anarchists and revolutionary syndicalists who used violent tactics.[17]

Although the IWW did adopt some syndicalist narratives, as they did of Marxism's class-conflict rhetoric, their goal of worker-controlled (rather than state-controlled) industries exhibits the distinguishing characteristic of the labor movement for the self-governing workshop. In 1913 a journalist asked an IWW member how to learn about the organization's history. The reply: "Study the Knights of Labor first, most of it is there."[18] The belief that labor creates wealth and therefore labor has a right to what it produces, in contrast to the "parasites" who appropriate wealth, was central to the IWW's moral philosophy. This example from a Pacific Northwest IWW newsletter in 1919 provides a glimpse of what producerist discursive strands looked like in the twentieth century: "That cloth you are weaving, the crops you are gathering, the mines you are delving into, the homes you are building, that good rich food you are transporting all belong to you. It is yours. By producing it you have gained the natural deed to it. . . . WORKERS OF AMERICA. Join the IWW. Show your contempt for the parasites who are living from your toil, by lining up in One Big Union. The parasites hate the IWW. Well they know that if the workers organize as a class it is the end of their robbery."[19]

Other narratives reminiscent of the self-governing workshop are apparent in notions of propertied independence, the relationship between economic resources and political liberty, and hostility to "the tyranny" of concentrated wealth and power. The newsletter continues:

No one is free who must depend on another for the privilege of earning their living. Of what use are political rights of free speech, assemblage, or any other expression if the right of individuals to an equal share or free access to the wealth of this earth is denied . . . it stands that in order to have real Democracy, we must first have the industries put on a Democratic basis, that is Industrial Democracy . . . [20]

Americanism to lie down under tyranny—that is merely Capitalized Americanism—and whereas the capitalist moralist teaches transcendent sanctity of servility, the IWW moralist teaches the noble duty of confounding and destroying tyranny. The IWW is the reembodiment of the spirit of Jefferson, Adams and Lincoln. Every true son and lover of liberty ought to comprehend that the abolition of the plutocrat and his reign is but the continuation of the early traditions of our country.[21]

As Seattle became the Northwest's industrial center by the second decade of the twentieth century, it became a stronghold for the IWW. The organization provided one explanation for the conditions of workers, as large populations of unemployed people came to Seattle. Although the economy was growing, it was outstripped by a continual surplus of labor. This problem was exacerbated by seasonal industries in mining, agriculture, and logging.

Hulet Wells, who would become a future participant in the general strike, articulated his experience of the transition in a single generation from an agrarian economy, with access to property and the fruits of one's labor, to the insecurity as a wage worker:

> As I grew up on the frontier there was no competition for jobs. Occasionally my father worked for someone else, getting paid in money or some other form of exchange, but mostly the pioneers worked for themselves, and on our homestead there was always plenty of work to do. . . . Willing workers might be sure of a living, for there was always soil and the soil was rich. . . . Unknown to me, however, an expanding capitalism was on the march, and the Northwest was too rich a prize to long escape the invasion. With it would come a strange new disease, the periodical plague of unemployment. . . . What was the cause of this amazing calamity? I could understand how it might happen to a poor country. . . . But here we had everything, rich soil, virgin forests, minerals, oil, coal and waterpower and plenty of capital, foreign and domestic.[22]

Wells's observation illustrates how the political economy of the United States, which readily provided access to land as a means of subsistence, forged the template for workplace democracy as the most resonant vision for the transformation of society. Liberty was experienced as direct worker control over resources, the production process, and created wealth. Narratives and practices of private ownership as the dominant organization of life and workplace independence constituted the identities of laborers well into the twentieth century. Workplace democracy was a *comprehensible* transition to an egalitarian industrial society because it previously constituted the experience of liberty, which was usurped within a lifetime or a few generations.

By 1910 the majority of Seattle's wage workers were unionized but mostly on a craft basis. Some employers claimed that Seattle was losing business because it was a "closed shop" town. The Seattle Chamber of Commerce publicly declared support for the open shop in 1914. They stated that "every effort possible should be made to maintain [the open shop] and the Chamber of Commerce pledges to use its influence towards that end."[23] The chamber was not aware of just how much work they had cut out for them.

THE WAR YEARS

In 1916 the American government took action to stimulate the shipbuilding industry through an act of Congress. Federal government assistance was to be provided for the establishment of a United States Shipping Board, which was formed in 1917. Although the board retained a supervisory function over all shipyard construction, the government agency responsible for construction was the Emergency Fleet Corporation (EFC), also established in 1917. To contend with problems of wage differentials and working conditions, the Shipbuilding Labor Adjustment Board (SLAB) was established by the EFC, which became known as the "Macy Board." The U.S. government neither owned nor operated the shipyards; private interests did this through government funds to create shipyards and to purchase ships. Seattle built roughly 26 percent of the ships contracted by the EFC.[24]

The United States Employment Service advised newly recruited workers to take out union cards. This was the result of the National War Labor Board's motto: "No strikes or lock-outs during the war." Essentially the government proposed a trade-off by guaranteeing that workers would not be fired for trade union activities in exchange for a no-strike pledge.[25] Furthermore, the Wilson administration was interested in addressing the conditions that produced labor strife and creating an alliance among "labor progressives, nonrevolutionary radicals and liberal democrats," who would support him in the 1916 presidential election.[26] By 1915 there were roughly fifteen thousand unionized workers in Seattle due to war-related increases in production. By 1917 this number had increased to forty thousand workers. By the end of the following year, there were sixty thousand union members in Seattle, mostly Euro-American men. Overall, there was an increase in union membership of approximately 300 percent within two and a half years.[27]

William Short, the president of the politically moderate Washington State AFL, expressed concerns about the problems associated with this influx of new members, many of whom had no history of union involvement. He noted that organizing was curtailed because the union lost many of its most experienced leaders through the Selective Service Act.[28] The new union members, mainly in shipbuilding and other war-related industries, were exempt from the selective service because of the status of these industries. Consequently these industries drew a good number of political radicals who opposed the war.

The increase in union density provided an organizational basis for more effective strikes, including general strikes. War production also dramatically increased the resources of labor. Increased resources during the war years—combined with this cultural stew of narratives and strategies from the Knights, the WFM, the ALU, and the IWW—created a flourishing workplace-democracy culture, the magnitude of which has rarely been seen since. This was apparent through the many proposals for economic and political transformation that emphasized worker ownership and worker management of industries, the most distinguishing characteristic of this political culture.

Given the prevalence of a producerist ethic, many workers felt they had a right to ownership and control of the industries as a matter of common sense. Harry Ault, the editor of the *Seattle Union Record* newspaper, stated that at the time the concept of "labor ownership of industry" was widespread.[29] He stated: "I believe that 95% of us agree that the workers should control the industries. Nearly all of us agree on that but very strenuously disagree on the method. Some of us think we can get it through the Cooperative movement, some of us think through political action, and others think through industrial action."[30] Regardless of the method, the desired transformation would put industries directly in the hands of working people rather than centralized state authority.

Producerist narratives and support for public ownership of utilities could even be found in the speeches of political officials in the early twentieth century. Consider the following record of congressional candidate speeches to Seattle unions from SCLC meeting minutes in 1919: "Mr. Rawson, candidate for Republican nomination spoke first and went on record for public ownership of public utilities, and stated that he was opposed to any person who took no part in the production of any article having any part of that which is produced [*sic*]. Col. C. M. Hawthorne, candidate for Democratic nomination, followed and went on record stating that he would always work for government ownership of the railroads, the telegraphs made part of our postal system, and government ownership of power resources."[31]

One avenue for workers to receive the fruits of their labor, proposed earlier by the Knights, was through labor-owned cooperatives. The first cooperative in Seattle, the "Mutual Laundry," was incorporated in 1915. There were soon other labor cooperatives, including stores, a bank, and the Labor Temple Association, with a fund of up to $75,000 contributed by roughly sixty local unions.[32] The SCLC organized a workers college. There were plans for creating a labor-owned bank and motion-picture company—the Union Label Film Company. The International Longshoremen's Association (ILA) planned to organize its own stevedoring company.

Cooperatives were one of labor's solutions to maintaining control over the workplace in an industrial capitalist economy. Some leaders proposed them as an intermediate step before industrial revolution or electoral transition to labor's ownership of industries. Others proposed cooperatives as a means to the eventual private control of the entire market by worker-owners. According to the Knights' vision of a cooperative commonwealth, with which working people in Seattle were familiar, the building of cooperatives for production and distribution was part of the road to the abolition of the wage system. As labor historian Selig Perlman suggested in 1928: "Consumer cooperatives were but a stepping stone to producers self employment [sic]. Eventually when the order had grown to include nearly all useful members of society . . . it would control practically the whole market."[33] The narratives used to promote worker cooperatives in Seattle were similar to those of the Knights in their two primary goals: (1) creating cooperatives for production and distribution to be "owned, managed and controlled by organized labor and farmers," and (2) reducing the cost of living by "withholding profits from the capitalist class" (see Figure 1).

Seattle labor consisted of three labor factions at the time: the progressives, the moderates, and the radicals. The first two groups organized most of the cooperatives.[34] The progressives were mostly reform socialists. They proposed public ownership of industries to be managed by the workers, similar to Debsian socialism. The progressives often participated in political coalitions with farmers and worked within the AFL to change its national policy from craft to industrial unionism. Anna Louise Strong, an editor and reporter for the *Seattle Union Record* at the time, described the characteristics of the progressives: "Within the movement I was considered one of the 'progressives,' which meant that I stood for industrial unionism (to be attained through a process of federating craft

ORGANIZED LABOR, READ THIS LETTER.
IT IS YOUR GREAT OPPORTUNITY.

TO THE MEMBERS OF ORGANIZED LABOR,
Seattle, Washington and Vicinity.

Fellow Workers:

Our object in writing to you at this time is to tell you of some of the achievements accomplished during the brief existence of The Co-Operative Food Products Association, since March, 1918. To secure the hearty co-operation of Organized Labor in a membership campaign. To secure a larger cash capital so that the Association can develope and extend its activities by increasing its present plants and equipments, and establishing branches in the most practical trading centers of the city, thus enabling it to serve more conveniently and with less expense its increasing patronage.

The Association, since it was organized in 1918, has accomplished the things it set out to do:

It fought the butchers' fight to a successful conclusion and kept down the prices of meats.

Through it the dairymen have sidestepped the milk trust by putting into operation a milk condensory to the mutual benefit of both Laborer and Farmer.

It has built and equipped a modern slaughter and packing house, and is now manufacturing its own meat products, to a large extent.

This Co-operative idea was promoted and carried out in the belief that by such an organization OWNED, MANAGED AND CONTROLLED by ORGANIZED LABOR AND FARMERS, food and eventually clothing, boots and shoes, and all other necessities and comforts of life, could be furnished to its members at more nearly the cost of production and distribution, than is done under the PRESENT PRIVATE PROFIT SYSTEM.

This Association is organized on the Rochdale plan and under such a system of co-operation;

It reduces the cost of living by withholding the profits from the capitalist class, and returning them to the purchaser as a consumer's dividend.

It places Labor in the position of being its own producer and distributor, thus acquiring the necessary knowledge and experience to the operation of the industry.

It aims to establish fair and equitable conditions in its methods of production and distribution, and finally saving to the worker the full social value of the services he renders to society, "the full product of his toil."

It is recreational, educational, and amalgamates the economic forces of the workers, thus enabling Labor to successfully combat the unfair tactics of the employer.

It is an ever ready ally, in case of strikes and lockouts, by having the commissary on the firing line, which will keep the wives and kiddies fed in these times of stress.

THE THING Organized Labor wants in Seattle is a modern Department Store, with its numerous branches and service stations, so that we can buy from ourselves, anything we may want, from a paper of pins or a cup of coffee, to a fine suit of clothes, a fine coat for the wife, an auttomobile or a $2.00 dinner. But we must creep before we run.

The Co-Operative Food Products Association has made a splendid financial success of its venture thus far. Its sales in the meat department have aggregated more than $1,250,000 since March, 1918, with splendid dividends to its member customers, on the purchases made.

The Association is now planning on enlarging its capacity and establishing branches to furnish all kinds of Food Products, including meats, groceries, provisions, fish, fruits and produce, to the workers as rapidly as the co-operation of the members of Organized Labor will permit, and is only awaiting the hearty response of a large number of Labor Unionists who do not now understand the co-operative movement and therefore are not as yet members.

To carry out this present program we must have at least $150,000.00 in additional paid-up capital, and to secure this we should have 5,000 new members, making personal cash capital subscriptions of from $10.00 to $1,000.00 each.

The Association, being composed only of organized Laborers and Farmers, wishes to state through its Organization Committee that this enterprise affords the members of the Seattle Labor Movement the greatest opportunity they have ever had to express their ideals in a concrete fashion, by owning and operating for their own use, benefit and pleasure the means of production and distribution of the necessities and comforts of life. Therefore, the Organization Committee is now planning an extensive and systematic campaign for new members in order that Organized Labor of Seattle and vicinity may realize the hopes and ideals for which they have yearned for years.

It expects to call upon each Local of Organized Labor in Seattle in the very near future to secure their hearty co-operation in obtaining subscriptions from their members toward the $150,000.00 needed at this time.

We earnestly urge that all Unions and their Officers grant representatives of the Committee a reasonable time at an early meeting of the Locals to more fully present this important matter to the members. In the meantime we ask that each Local urge its members to come to the Organization Committee Office of The Co-Operative Food Products Association, at the South End Market and make their subscription for as much stock as they can purchase, so that they may become beneficiary members as soon as possible. The Committee will appreciate the courtesy and thank you on behalf of Organized Labor.

Fraternally.

ORGANIZATION COMMITTEE,

FRED NELSON,
R. D. No. 5, Seattle, Wash.

O. P. CALLAHAN,
2528 Yale Avenue, Seattle, Wash.

C. E. STEAD,
415 West 73rd, Seattle, Wash.

Organized Labor: Read This Letter, University of Washington

FIG 1. *"Organized Labor, Read This Letter. It Is Your Great Opportunity." Cooperative Food Products Association flyer, 1919. From Broussais Beck papers, Acc. 0155-001, 0155-002, 0155-003, Box 2, Folder 16, University of Washington Libraries, Special Collections.*

unions), for political action by labor (we were developing a farmer-labor party against the reactionaries of the American Federation of Labor) and for eventual rule by the workers, without specifying how or when."[35]

Most of the officials on the SCLC were progressives. Although the council affiliated with the AFL, James Duncan, their representative, consistently voted against the reelection of the moderate Samuel Gompers as AFL president. The moderates were drawn mostly from skilled workers and identified with the AFL's bread-and-butter unionism. Their orientation was most similar to union officials like William Short, the president of the Washington State Federation of Labor (WSFL), and Samuel Gompers, the president of the national AFL. They respected capitalism and the right of nonproductive capitalists to profit from their labor, but they demanded a "fair wage for a fair day's work." The moderates tended to be more left-leaning than their counterparts in other regions. In the same way that the AFL pulled the Socialist Party to the right in the United States, the workplace-democracy political culture in Seattle, with its greater representation of IWW members and reform socialists, pulled their AFL craft unionists to the left.

The radicals, the third faction among Seattle labor, tended to be less skilled and were concentrated in the metal trades and shipyard unions. (The term "radical" means simply that this group sought the most deep-rooted change of society.) Many of these activists were IWW members, their sympathizers, or revolutionary socialists who believed in some type of immediate revolutionary change, rather than in slow reform through the electoral system. The IWW argued that labor needed to work outside the political system because capitalists controlled the state. The general strike was to be the means through which labor directly gained control of industries. Consequently they encouraged militant direct action to gain concessions and education to provide employees with the skills for eventual management of society. They supported forming One Big Union of all workers on a class, not craft, basis. They were inclusive of nationality, race, gender, and age (including children who worked in factories).

Within Seattle's political culture the discourses of the progressives and radicals exhibited continuities with those of the nineteenth-century movement for the self-governing workshop. Despite some similarities among the goals and strategies of the IWW and the reform socialists, there were also important differences between them.[36] Socialists sought state ownership of the means of production with worker management, whereas the IWW sought direct ownership and control of industries by the workers themselves. Reform socialists thought they could create change through the electoral system, whereas the syndicalists argued that the state was a tool of the capitalists and therefore the electoral system was not capable of revolutionary transformation.

The *Seattle Union Record*, the first daily labor newspaper in the United States, established in 1918 by the SCLC (thanks to increased labor resources), also contributed to a vibrant labor culture. It resembled other major dailies in its layout: articles, editorials, fashion, and cartoons. At one point the paper out-circulated the *Seattle Star*, one of the city's leading dailies. The *Seattle Union Record* was an important network for the communication of workplace-democracy narratives among laborers, but the organization of laborers' communities, workplaces, unions, and cooperatives comprised other networks. Seattle's workers resided throughout the city, and these organizations and institutions "reigned in meaning" that was generated through shared experiences and available cultural material.[37] Working-class neighborhoods were spatially organized in ways similar to most cities at this time: "differentiated along occupational lines . . . the upper stratum of organized labor and the lower middle class tended to congregate in the cities, valleys and flatlands," with unskilled and transient labor concentrated in the downtown area.[38]

Given the workplace-democracy inclinations of Seattle labor, its increased resources and power alarmed employers and some middle-class sympathizers. Of particular concern were the new workers drawn to the metal trades, many of whom were known to be labor militants. Anxieties were amplified through the polarizing effect of World War I, producing both radicals and hyperpatriots in its wake. Although Seattle workers profited from war-related production, the SCLC leaders openly opposed the war. When the United States officially entered the war on April 6, the council sent a telegram of protest to the federal government. At the same time the city's Municipal League announced that "the time for debate is over . . . we will encourage others to be loyal and stamp out disloyalty wherever we may find it." The league requested that the governor call a special session of the legislature so it could define acts that hinder war production, like strikes. An internment camp for the disloyal was also proposed.[39]

Despite increased unionization during the war, unions were constrained by the no-strike pledge made by national AFL officials. Seattle labor was not in agreement over this pledge. The political culture exhibited an unusually strong ethos of rank-and-file control within the union, which was fueled by disdain for centralized authority, both of which were workplace-democracy characteristics. Most Seattle unions wanted the rank and file to vote for the pledge through referendums. Because they did not vote on this agreement, they should not be held accountable to it. This dispute was one example of the tensions among national AFL officials, who felt empowered to make such decisions on behalf of the rank and file, and local workplace-democracy practices of participatory democracy within the union.

Public opposition to the war also increased the existing strains between the SCLC and the WSFL. Short, WSFL's president, was a close protégé of Gompers, the moderate president of the AFL. Both men supported the war. In 1918, Short was reelected as WSFL president without the support of Seattle locals, a sign of the growing isolation of the SCLC from organized labor in the state.[40]

As America finally joined the war, hyperpatriotism among the less complex thinkers of the world translated into attacks on anyone perceived as "disloyal." In 1917 the IWW called for a massive strike in the lumber industry on July 17. By midsummer large numbers of their Lumber Workers Industrial Union and the AFL's Brotherhood of Timber Workers participated in the strike. It devastated the lumber industry and impeded war production. The police swept through IWW camps and charged the offenders with such petty offenses as "vagrancy" and "using profane language." The Department of Justice joined with the Seattle police in raiding IWW halls on September 6. After this raid the Seattle police department joined with federal officials in other raids that violated the civil liberties of IWW members through searches without warrants and improper arrests.[41]

Vigilantism by self-described "patriots" continued to rise. The Minutemen of Seattle, who called themselves "the Men Behind the Government," disrupted IWW and socialist gatherings. They worked with federal authorities by reporting "suspicious" persons. As their records state: "Have listed and have reports upon 1100 dangerous IWW and 8000 others. Have arranged for advice on movements of IWW coming here from Mining camps in Rockies. Are checking Payrolls of industrialists.

Arranging for daily reports through employment agencies. Our men are detailed along the waterfront, in IWW and in Shipyards. We co-operate with and follow directions of Federal Departments on IWW, aliens, sedition, slackers, Food and Fuel laws. We boil case down ready for prosecution."[42]

The antiwar stand taken by the Socialist Party and the IWW destroyed the prewar alliances of the Progressive Era and divided the community into "patriots" (those who supported the war) and the "reds" (those who opposed it).[43] To add fuel to the fire, the majority of Seattle workers supported the Bolshevik revolution in 1917, in sharp contrast to the "patriots." The SCLC was jubilant at the success of the revolution, in which workers gained control of their industries. The *Seattle Union Record* vehemently opposed intervention against the new "workers state" and printed numerous articles and editorials on postrevolutionary developments in Russia. The WSFL was much more cautious in its response.

President Woodrow Wilson, feeling strongly that the growth of Bolshevism had to be stopped in order to preserve the free market, was committed to fight against it both internationally and internally. Such views indirectly affected the level of police repression against the IWW and other "radicals."[44] Closely timed to the Bolshevik revolution in November were police raids on the Seattle IWW and Socialist offices in concert with vigilantes.[45] In 1918 mayoral candidate Ole Hanson ran a hyper-patriot campaign for mayor of Seattle and won. That same year the Department of Justice sent a representative to oversee the prosecution of detainees accused of violating the Espionage Act; numerous IWW members were among them. But, ironically, the steps taken to repress the IWW facilitated one of the conditions that contributed to the general strike—an increase in the number of radical industrial unionists in Seattle. The Department of Labor ordered a roundup of "alien" radicals in the Pacific Northwest. By the summer of 1918 the IWW had been driven out of the woods, and many of its members moved to nearby cities to find jobs. As Seattle historian Richard C. Berner has suggested: "The result in Seattle was the infusion of more militants into an already radical-leaning union work force."[46]

In this polarized atmosphere some members of the business community were quick to seize the opportunity to discredit Seattle labor as un-American. Shipyard employers shared social networks with the owners of most Seattle newspapers. Both the *Seattle Times* and the *Seattle Star* expressed antilabor views; the business counterweight to labor's *Seattle Union Record* was Edwin Selvin's *Business Chronicle of the Pacific Northwest*. Selvin was a public spokesperson for employer interests whose rhetorical attacks on a labor "riot" (a mass meeting that was broken up by the police) in 1919 illustrate the polarization of the time:

> "Hail to the Bolsheviki! Hail to the revolution! Our system of government must change!" So one of the Bolshevik propagandists at large in America closed his inflammatory harangue, made publicly, on the streets of Seattle, last Sunday. . . .

> Cries of, "The revolution starts today!" . . . "The damned employers will get theirs now!" "Hang every rich man!" "Confiscate wealth!" . . . brought forth prolong[ed] cheers. . . . Business Men and Property Owners! Awake to the peril that is infinitely more awful than the Hun, and that is even now at your gates.[47]

The equation of employees who challenged workplace disempowerment with "traitors" and business interests with "patriotism" was common in Seattle newspapers. In January 1919 the Washington State Legislature passed an antisyndicalism bill that was signed into law by the governor.

The daily publication of the *Seattle Union Record* provided labor with the means to respond to these attacks. The editors emphasized its support for the war effort, but letters to the editor criticizing the war were also printed. Support of the war did not, however, draw on the framing of hyperpatriotism that was common to the other leading dailies. Refracting their social locations, the *Seattle Union Record* editors valorized producerism and challenged concentrated wealth and power. Editorials claimed that labor had done the "REAL WORK in order that victory might be ours." Fighting a "war for democracy as opposed to autocracy" was a common theme within the daily's pages and was drawn on to justify labor's demand for industrial democracy.[48]

THE PRELUDE: THE METAL TRADES STRIKE

In 1919, *The Nation* magazine wrote about the worldwide rank-and-file revolt fueled in part by the Russian revolution.[49] There was a communist revolt in Germany and a revolution in Hungary, as well as general strikes in Argentina, Chile, and Peru. The United States experienced a wave of postwar strikes that often challenged both the AFL hierarchy and autocratic managers within the workplace.

Aside from the inspiration of the world's first "workers state," several conditions contributed to the labor protests that occurred throughout the country. First, industries had been experiencing changes in workplace organization through the "scientific management" promoted by Frederick Taylor. These changes involved acute specialization, time and motion management, and discipline within the production process. Second, challenges to "autocratic" management were fueled by previous experiences of labor autonomy. Many people, including numerous immigrants, had experienced the transition from agricultural production (in which they had control over the labor process) to wage worker within one or two generations, as Hulet Wells had in Seattle. They knew life could be different. Finally, as scholar Joseph A. McCartin has pointed out, labor and progressives were encouraged by President Woodrow Wilson's war labor policies. By January 1919 national AFL membership hit a peak of 3.2 million, one million more than in 1917.[50]

In the postwar years the term "workers control," rarely used prior to this era, became common within labor circles. These were the decades of what labor scholars David Montgomery has called the "new unionism," Christopher Tomlins and others have called the "culture of control," and McCartin has termed "industrial democracy."[51] Notably, the *Seattle Union Record* covered these events and communicated this zeitgeist.

In the United States the demobilization of troops produced thousands of unemployed people needing work in American cities. A January 1919 article in the *Seattle Union Record* quoted Secretary of Labor Wilson urging Congress to pass both the Kelly Bill and the Kenyan Bills, appropriating funds for government projects that would provide jobs. Wilson warned Congress that jobs were needed to avert the "unemployment danger" and to keep working people from "IWW doctrines" and the "philosophy of force."[52]

Assistant Secretary of Labor Louis F. Post expressed concern over the plight of working people. Drawing on producerist narratives that equated concentrated wealth and absentee owners with exploitation, he publicly argued against criticisms that wage laborers indulged in extortion and profiteering when they organized into unions. Post hinted at the labor theory of value: "Men whose annual wages would hardly pay the annual theater expenses of a gentleman of leisure cannot be accused of extortion. . . . What possible powers of extortion do wage workers have? Unorganized, they have none at all. These workers cannot get even what are called 'fair wages' except as their organized fellow workers standardize wages. And organized wage workers can standardize wages only by quitting work in bodies or threatening to do so if fair wages are refused. . . . Wage workers engaged in production do not get what they earn. And when it comes to extortion, what about highway corporations and their watered stock? What about water power monopolies? What about timber barons? What about monopolizers of natural deposits—coal, iron, oil, copper?"[53] Despite Post's appeals to not lower wages, organized employers and government officials were intent on doing just that.

Because of strong unions and increased shipyard wages during the war, the wage standards in Seattle were higher than in other sections of the country. At that time the cost of living also increased. Workers in Seattle tended to pay higher rents because of housing shortages that increased with the influx of new workers from other parts of the country. During the war the Seattle shipyards had negotiated closed-shop collective bargaining contracts through the shipyard owners and the Metal Trades Council, consisting of delegates from seventeen craft unions. Due to the preference for industrial unionism, the SCLC negotiated a single blanket agreement made at intervals for all metal trades crafts. By August 1917 the Metal Trades Council negotiated a uniform wage scale for about one-third of the workers. Other unions had contracts with clauses that required the consent of the government for wage increases.

At this time the Macy Board adjusted wages for the duration of the war. But instead of creating greater wage uniformity, the adjustment resulted in gross wage inequalities among shipyard workers. Many workers were angry because this action undermined years of labor struggles to obtain their current wage scales. The resentment was exacerbated by the fact that the AFL International officers had signed the memorandum creating the Macy Board, which obligated the workers, who believed in rank-and-file control, to its decision without a referendum vote.[54]

With the war in process, the metal trades union agreed to stay on the job while negotiations continued. The Macy Board deadlocked on the appeal decision, but the representatives of the Metal Trades Council left with a personal assurance from Charles Piez, chairman of the EFC, that unions could negotiate directly with the employers once the war was over.

Negotiations continued. Seattle workers assumed that these negotiations would eventually result in pay raises.

Following the signing of the armistice in November 1918, the Macy Board made its announcement for adjusting wage scales to absorb increased war costs. Wages were to be increased in almost every sector of the shipbuilding industry but the Puget Sound District, where wages did not increase and in some types of work the wages were in fact cut. Furthermore, wages were set as maximum rather than minimum amounts. The Macy Board said that it had reduced Puget Sound wages because Seattle shipyard owners lured workers away from other ports. According to Piez, this loss was disrupting the entire program of the EFC in the West, as workers from shipyards in Portland and San Francisco moved to Seattle.[55]

The Macy Board's decision to lessen wage differentials in the shipbuilding industries was met with surprise and anger among Seattle unions and among sympathizers within the community. As noted earlier, adhering to the board's decisions in the first place had been questioned by metal trades workers, who charged that the international officers had no authority to bind their locals to this agreement without a referendum vote. The attempt of the EFC to standardize wages meant reducing Seattle wages to those applied to regions run under open-shop employers. Organized labor was concerned that this was a first step toward the eventual destruction of their unions.[56]

In response, meetings were held among unions, employers, and sympathetic religious groups. Together they sent a recommendation to Piez requesting that the Macy Board's decision be amended to increase wages in the Puget Sound area. Representatives were sent to Washington, D.C., to make an appeal on behalf of the Metal Trades Council. William Short, president of the WSFL, recounted that with the endorsement of the employers and community support to increase wages, most presumed that the government board would concede. Meanwhile, the cost of living in Seattle continued to increase. In November, following the signing of the armistice, the shipyard workers called for a strike vote, which was approved after a ballot count on December 10.

Once the rank and file approved the strike, the next step was to approach the employers to negotiate a contract. The owners responded in January 1919 with an offer to increase the wages of the skilled mechanics only. Because of workplace-democracy resonance for One Big

Union, however, Seattle labor concluded that it was an attempt to divide the skilled from the unskilled and undermine solidarity. The offer was rejected, although this type of contract was accepted by moderate AFL craft unions nationwide.

Piez claimed that the strike violated the recent agreement made with the Labor Adjustment Board, which was to run until March 31, 1919.[57] Seattle labor felt that they had been deceived. In response, union representatives claimed that, yes, they had appealed to the Macy Board but that the appeal had resulted in a deadlock. The *Seattle Union Record* explained: "The Metal Trades were told that they could negotiate directly with the shipyard owners. The delegates came back here and opened negotiations, extending over a period of several weeks in length. Before the ship owners would enter into these negotiations they communicated with the Macy Board and were told they might go ahead. Those negotiations failed. A strike followed."[58]

In the midst of these developments, Piez covertly sent telegraphs to the shipowners telling them not to give in to union demands or they would have their steel allotments cut back and government contracts would be canceled.[59] But an interesting twist of fate occurred. The telegram from Piez was "accidentally" delivered to the Metal Trades Council (the workers) rather than to the intended Metal Trades Association (the employers). Seattle unionists were outraged. The *Seattle Union Record* claimed that Piez had used "underhanded methods" and his actions constituted "a direct challenge to the organized labor movement of the Northwest." Piez's duplicity and breach of state neutrality had to be challenged. Many workers thought that he was trying to undermine the power of organized labor and the gains they had made during the war. Their concern materialized in the form of a shipyard strike that began on January 21, 1919. Roughly thirty-five thousand metal trades employees participated.[60] As a show of solidarity with Puget Sound workers, Tacoma shipyard workers also went out that day.

The newspaper coverage of the shipyard strike was mostly negative, with the *Seattle Times* pointing out that workers were losing a million dollars of wages a week. A letter to the editor in the *Seattle Union Record* responded to this charge with a producerist argument: "We would like to ask how the workers are losing anything of wages. The workers are the producers of all the wealth that has the origin in the shipyards as well as elsewhere. When the workers are producing wealth, by the process of working, they produce more than they receive in return as wages. Consequently, they are losing part of their produce every day they work. . . . When they cease production they cannot lose anything for the simple reason that when not producing they have nothing to lose."[61]

In response to the strike, shipyard owner David Skinner sent a wire to Piez claiming that the workmen did not favor the strike but were forced into it by radical leadership. This had been picked up by wire services, and Skinner made this claim in front of local audiences. Piez's office sent out bulletins trying to persuade the American public that revolutionaries were behind the shipyard strike. Letters to the editor appeared in major newspapers claiming to be from workers who opposed the strike.

To counter these accusations, the union called for a mass meeting on January 26 at the Hippodrome. In attendance were roughly six thousand Boilermakers of Local 104, the largest union on strike. The motion to endorse the strike was carried by a unanimous standing vote. The next day the *Seattle Union Record* described this gathering as "probably the largest and most enthusiastic meeting of organized labor which has been held in the Northwest." The unanimous vote taken at this meeting enhanced support for a general strike.[62]

Some Seattle newspapers cautioned that it was bad timing to have a strike against the shipbuilding industry because the war had just ended and thus there was a reduced need for ships. The *Seattle Union Record* responded by arguing that "the gap that the war made in the world's shipping has not yet been filled, and American Capital has a golden harvest yet to reap in filling it. If the present owners don't care to get rich filling the world's demand for ships there are plenty of other capitalists who will willingly take their places. . . . Don't be afraid that the work is going to be done in another part of the country. . . . The people who buy ships are buyers in the market the same as you, and necessity compels them to buy in the cheapest market. The Puget Sound district can build ships cheaper than any other place in the United States. There are ships to be built and they will be built right here. We call their bluff."[63] This article also encouraged workers to do business with the union-owned food cooperatives because the Seattle Retail Grocers Association had curtailed credit for the strikers. When the union-owned Cooperative Food Products Association tried to provide support, police raided its offices, claiming that they were looking for illegal liquor.[64]

The SCLC used the *Seattle Union Record* to appeal to the pubic, especially small merchants, to support the shipyard strike. Two themes were prominent in these mobilization appeals. The first involved the benefits to the community and to local businesses when wages are higher. From the January 30, 1919, issue of the *Seattle Union Record*: "Regarding the present metal trades strike in this city, where does your interest lie? In the hands of the shipyard owners or in the fate of the worker in the strike? If the strike is won, it will mean a distribution of $200,000 to $300,000 a week among the businessmen of Seattle. If we lose, can or will the shipyard owners distribute that much money among the small businessmen of Seattle? Think it over and see if your interest is with or against the worker in this struggle."[65]

The second appeal involved the injustice of exorbitant profits made by the shipowners. In the nineteenth and early twentieth centuries ethical notions of "unjust accumulation" of capitalists could still be found in public discourses, but these became muted in the latter part of the twentieth century. During the war there were strong feelings of hostility toward industrialists who reaped huge war profits. Building on this resentment, the *Seattle Union Record* emphasized these concerns: "Tuesday afternoon the *Union Record* published a statement issued by Bert Swain, secretary of the Seattle Metal Trades Council, showing tremendous profits that were being made by the shipbuilding firms. It was pointed out that the increased wage requested could be paid and still leave big profits for the employer. The figures submitted by Mr. Swain have been verified and their accuracy hasn't been denied."[66] During the metal trades strike numerous small merchants supported the wage laborers and continued to be their allies throughout the general strike.

THE GENERAL STRIKE

After the armistice the SCLC turned its attention to the Tom Mooney case. Mooney was a labor activist who had been convicted of throwing a bomb in a 1916 Preparedness Day parade in San Francisco. Evidence showed that he was innocent, however. In November 1918 the SCLC voted to hold a referendum on the question of calling a national general strike on Mooney's behalf. The SCLC locals were strongly in favor of it. The Tom Mooney Defense League organized a National Labor Congress in Chicago on January 14, 1919, to strategize.

As the metal trades strike progressed, the moderate WSFL president,

William Short, expressed concerns about developments in Seattle in a letter to AFL president Samuel Gompers. Short concluded that the IWW had become so influential among Seattle labor that the SCLC was "determined to have a general strike, if not over 'Mooney,' then [sic] they will attempt it over something else."[67] On January 22, while the SCLC officials were away in Chicago, the president of the Metal Trades Council proposed a general strike resolution for referendum vote at the SCLC meeting. It was "overwhelmingly passed."

The meeting was dominated by the metal trades unions, many of whom were dual-card IWW members or sympathizers. Historian Robert L. Freidheim has described the event: "[It] was a wild, tumultuous affair. Charles W. Doyle, acting secretary of the Council, found himself unable to maintain a smooth, orderly flow of business. He had to pound his gavel frequently to quiet the spectators in the packed galleries—Wobblies, according to the *Star*—who again and again disrupted the speeches on the floor by shouting, clapping and singing. The delegates themselves behaved little better. There were emotional appeals for the Seattle labor movement to cast itself adrift from the AFL and reorganize on the industrial union plan. Pandemonium broke loose when the Metal Trades Council requested the general strike referendum."[68]

The next-day support for the general strike "began to snowball." The enthusiasm for having a general strike becomes comprehensible given the zeitgeist of the times. As mentioned earlier, the general strike occurred in the midst of a national strike wave after World War I, with revolts and general strikes erupting internationally. Only two years earlier the Russian revolution had established the first "workers state." One participant in the Seattle general strike explained that "perhaps now it [the general strike] seems astonishing, but in post-Armistice Seattle it was natural and inevitable—this great emotional wave."[69] *Seattle Union Record* editor and reporter Anna Louise Strong commented that "the sight of workers seizing power in other countries had stirred their emotions and aroused a faith that some day it might be their turn to supersede the capitalists in managing the world. Now suddenly [during the general strike] they had to manage."[70]

Both the media and the public were surprised at the amount of support the general strike referendum generated. SCLC officials met concerning the proposed general strike when they returned from Chicago. Many were ambivalent if not directly opposed to it. Strong concluded that if the labor leaders had been at the meeting, the strike would never have taken place.[71] But SCLC officials respected the workplace-democracy practice of rank-and-file decision making. Since there was no way to stop the referendum, they agreed to go along with the majority decision.[72]

SCLC representatives decided that the strike would be "sympathetic," not a "mass" one, which some argued for. In a "mass" strike all unions would have listed grievances and stayed out until they were met. The SCLC opted instead for a demonstration of solidarity for other workers. The Metal Trades Council created a colored poster to represent the spirit of the strike. It portrayed a soldier, a sailor, and a worker in overalls with the motto: "TOGETHER WE WIN."

A variety of unions voted in favor of the general strike, including the Milk Wagon Drivers, the Musicians, the Hog Carriers and Laborers, the Teamsters, the Plumbers, the Hotel Maids, the Longshoremen, the Housepainters and Decorators, and the Typographers. The electricians, "lady barbers," and cigar makers were unanimous in their support. Initially the only opposition to the general strike came from the Gas Workers and the Federal Employees Union (FEU). The FEU stated that they opposed "that radical element seeking to tear down and destroy what the Central Labor Council and the American Federation of Labor had been 20 years in building up."[73] One hundred and ten unions in all voted to strike, including the carpenters, perhaps the most conservative union in Seattle. Because of racist restrictions, Japanese unions could not have representatives on the SCLC, but despite this, they sent two delegates to tell the council that they would also strike.[74] They were admitted to meetings in a participatory but nonvoting role.[75]

The first meeting of the General Strike Committee on February 2 occurred four days prior to the general strike. The strike was democratically organized. Authority for general strike decisions passed from the SCLC to a committee of more than three hundred members, who were elected from 110 local unions and the SCLC. Due to organizational considerations the General Strike Committee delegated power to a smaller committee of fifteen people. The Committee of Fifteen held authority over most decisions, including the decision of which industries would continue to provide services and which would not. Both committees were involved in lengthy daily meetings throughout the duration of the general strike. Shifting responsibility from the SCLC to the General Strike Committee was tactically advantageous. It facilitated a sense of participation among the rank and file and undermined the attempts of the internationals to stop the strike via threats to revoke the SCLC's charter. But the formation of a new committee lacking administrative experience created tensions as a result of the massive responsibilities of coordinating a general strike without prior experience.

In the midst of these developments the unions attempted to build coalitions with farmers. Organized labor and farming associations had engaged in cooperative ventures in the past, such as the Farmers Union and the Triple Alliance. A *Seattle Union Record* editorial drew on workplace-democracy narratives to appeal to farmers as fellow producers:

> How often have we heard the remark that farmers and plain workers for wages must depend upon the so-called upper classes for leadership! . . . Yet in the past three years these intelligent classes have so brazenly failed to protect the sheep that even the dullest-witted sheep can see the failure. . . . What farmer, for instance, would be so foolish as to fix the price on wheat and let prices on what the farmer has to buy run wild? What farmer would fail to act if he were in congress to end the vicious packing trust monopoly exposed by the trade commission? What farmer or workingman would be so absurd as to keep the taxes on freight, express and first class mail and lower it on war profits and swollen incomes? . . . Instead of looking after the sheep [the upper classes] are raising wool and selling mutton.[76]

Labor solidarity inclusive of the skilled and unskilled, race, and gender—a legacy of the Knights—was about to be tested through the general strike. Unionists were sensitive to employer attempts to create labor divisions, but Seattle unions were not immune to the culture of contradictions that continued to permeate American institutions into the twentieth century. As has been pointed out, this is a result of the contradictory logic, apparent to the founders and embedded within American culture, of rhetoric emphasizing equality, liberty, and inclusion combined with practices of exclusion based on race and gender. Workplace-democracy narratives that emphasized equality and inclusion provided a greater cultural opportunity to empower people of color and women within the union than did the narratives and practices of moderate craft unionism. Nevertheless during the general strike solidarity was constructed, for the most part, as a male Euro-American project.[77]

Seattle had a small population of African Americans, roughly 1 percent in 1920, and there was one African American on the General Strike Committee in 1919. Unions that participated in the shipyard strike and the Seattle general strike had few people of color in them, and the African Americans who worked in the shipyards were limited to the most undesirable jobs. They were excluded from most Seattle unions and relegated to jobs considered "proper" for their race, mostly service positions. The longshoremen at the port of Seattle were a notable exception. Consequently the experiences and narratives of African-American workers were, for the most part, silenced within the SCLC because of their lack of resources and power within the union and the larger community.

There was a greater inclusion of women in Seattle's workplace-democracy culture. Without doubt, the labor culture was patriarchal, with minimal challenges to traditional gender subordination.[78] The narratives often equated workplace democracy with manhood. Yet Euro-American women's access to resources facilitated their greater participation within Seattle's labor movement than that of people of color. The first type of resource was territorial-based suffrage in the late nineteenth century. Progressives pursued electoral strategies that increased the status of women as voters. There were numerous labor-owned cooperatives through which women were involved in union consumption campaigns.[79] Women did outreach and encouraged community members to buy through cooperatives and respect the union label. Also, the workplace-democracy inclination for large industrial unions rendered women's positions within workplaces more salient in order to unionize all workers in an industry; for example, most telephone operators were Euro-American women.

Women commonly spoke at union and political meetings as labor organizers, workers, relatives of workers, and representatives for union labels and cooperative consumption. The radical Kate Sadler spoke at numerous mass meetings. The aforementioned editor and reporter Anna Louise Strong was influential among rank-and-file workers, especially among IWW members.[80] A number of women were elected to the General Strike Committee. Despite their greater presence than in some labor cultures, women's perspectives and experiences, especially those of working-class feminists, were marginalized. Nevertheless, the women's unions—the hotel maids, laundry workers, and lady barbers among others—did participate. The History Committee of the General Strike Committee noted that during the general strike the women's unions "showed a strong feeling of loyalty towards the strike, many of them out-lasting the men of the same craft."[81]

Most Seattle newspapers presented the general strike from the per-spectives of employers and political officials. The conservative *Seattle Times* wrote about the "Bolsheviki Plan to Turn Back to Era of Savagery" and applauded U.S. troops sent to Russia to overthrow the Bolsheviks. Not surprisingly, it assailed the general strike as the work of "radicals." On February 2 the *Seattle Times* argued that workers had been forced into idleness despite their desire not to strike. Articles about how the gen-eral strike resulted from radicals attempting to promote revolution filled the press. The people of Seattle proceeded to stock up on supplies and groceries. The press reported that some wealthy families had left the city for the duration of the strike. By February 3 leaflets had gone up around the city written by the IWW declaring that "Russia Did It," which encour-aged workers to take control of the industries (see Figure 2). Although this was not an official declaration by the Metal Trades Council or the SCLC, it fed conservative fears that the strike had a revolutionary inten-tion. As a testimony to the postwar polarization, while workers were put-ting up these flyers, two Minutemen "arrested them."[82]

The *Seattle Union Record* never encouraged a revolutionary general strike, although some letters to the editor discussed revolutionary goals. It did, however, provide a vehicle for the expression of workplace-democracy principles like the labor theory of value and the right of labor-ers to the wealth they produced. The newspaper communicated the belief that the dignity of Americans comes through the intelligent and dem-ocratic management of their own labor. It publicized the insurrections of workers around the world who had challenged the theft of labor's wealth and power by the nonproducing class of absentee owners, fin-anciers, and monopolists. This zeitgeist was apparent in journalist Strong's "No One Knows Where" column, printed on February 4, which was singled out as evidence that the general strike was revolutionary. This piece, excerpted below, has been called the most quoted editorial in Seat-tle newspaper history:

We are undertaking the most tremendous move ever taken
by LABOR in this country, a move which will lead
NO ONE KNOWS WHERE! . . .
LABOR WILL FEED THE PEOPLE

RUSSIA DID IT

SHIPYARD WORKERS—You left the shipyards to enforce your demands for higher wages. Without you your employers are helpless. Without you they cannot make one cent of profit—their whole system of robbery has collapsed.

The shipyards are idle; the toilers have withdrawn even tho the owners of the yards are still there. Are your masters building ships? No. Without your labor power it would take all the shipyard employers of Seattle and Tacoma working eight hours a day the next thousand years to turn out one ship. Of what use are they in the shipyards?

It is you and you alone who build the ships; you create all the wealth of society today; you make possible the $75,000 sable coats for millionaires' wives. It is you alone who can build the ships.

They can't build the ships. You can. Why don't you?

There are the shipyards; more ships are urgently needed; you alone can build them. If the masters continue their dog-in-the-manger attitude, not able to build the ships themselves and not allowing the workers to, there is only one thing left for you to do.

Take over the management of the shipyards yourselves; make the shipyards your own; make the jobs your own; decide the working conditions yourselves; decide your wages yourselves.

In Russia the masters refused to give their slaves a living wage too. The Russian workers put aside the bosses and their tool, the Russian government, and took over industry in their own interests.

There is only one way out; a nation-wide general strike with its object the overthrow of the present rotten system which produces thousands of millionaires and millions of paupers each year.

The Russians have shown you the way out. What are you going to do about it? You are doomed to wage slavery till you die unless you wake up, realize that you and the boss have not one thing in common, that the employing class must be overthrown, and that you, the workers, must take over the control of your jobs, and thru them, the control over your lives instead of offering yourselves up to the masters as a sacrifice six days a week, so that they may coin profits out of your sweat and toil.

71

FIG 2. *"Russia Did It." From the Industrial Workers of the World, Seattle Office Records, Acc. 544, Box 3, University of Washington Libraries, Special Collections.*

Twelve great kitchens have been offered, and from them food
will be distributed by the provision trades at low cost to all.
LABOR WILL CARE FOR THE BABIES AND THE SICK.
The milk-wagon drivers and the laundry drivers are arranging
plans for supplying milk to babies, invalids and hospitals,
and taking care of the cleaning of linen for hospitals.
LABOR WILL PRESERVE ORDER.
The strike committee is arranging for guards, and it is expected
that the stopping of the cars will keep people at home. . . .
Labor will not only SHUT DOWN the industries, but Labor will REOPEN under
the management of the appropriate trades, such activities as [these] are
needed to preserve public health and public peace. If the strike continues,
Labor may feel led to avoid public suffering by reopening more and more
activities.
UNDER ITS OWN MANAGEMENT.
And that is why we say that we are starting on a road that leads
—NO ONE KNOWS WHERE.[83]

Whether this piece communicates revolutionary intent or not, it does
communicate a workplace-democracy model of egalitarian transformation among labor and capital through direct worker ownership and control of industries. The radical factions, especially the IWW, would have
welcomed this model of revolutionary transformation. In fact, on February 5 revolutionary socialists proposed a resolution stating that if the
employers refused to grant concessions, the workers should take control of the shipbuilding.[84]

The resolution did not pass. But its presentation at the meeting was
consistent with the long history of competing political factions and tensions within the Seattle labor movement. Although the overall political
culture exhibited workplace-democracy characteristics, the progressives, as noted earlier, tended to support electoral reform, not revolution, and they were heavily represented on the SCLC. Only a small
minority of the radical faction of syndicalists and revolutionary socialists entertained the thought that the Seattle general strike could be a
vehicle for revolution, but they were not in leadership positions. While
the lack of revolutionary intent was apparent to the unions involved, this
was not so clear to the employers and city officials.

On the same day that the "No One Knows Where" column appeared in the newspapers, a citizens committee was formed, led by the president of Seattle's Chamber of Commerce. Public anxiety increased because of a statement made by William Green, the business agent of the Electrical Workers local, that City Light (a city-owned provider of electrical energy) would be shut down. Green apparently had no authority to speak. In fact, the General Strike Committee had no plans to shut it down and felt that there weren't enough organized workers to do it even if they wanted to. But the press seized on Green's statement.[85]

On Thursday, February 6, 1919, sixty thousand AFL workers walked off the job when the 10 A.M. whistle blew, and several thousand IWW members joined them. Roughly forty thousand laborers who were not officially on strike did not report to work that day for various reasons. Some could not get to work, or their employers saw no reason to open the business, and still others were wary of a possible "revolutionary uprising."[86]

Beginning with the first day, rumors ran rampant. The primary means of communication for labor—the newspapers, meetings, street gatherings, and information from coworkers—had been cut off. The *Seattle Union Record* stopped printing on February 6 and began again on February 8. This made it difficult to substantiate or deny the rumors. Historian Murray Morgan has described what happened that first day:

After the ten o'clock whistle sounded merchants and lawyers and tradesmen and workers stood anxiously in front of their shops and offices, waiting for what was to come. The minutes stretched into hours and nothing happened. A hearse rolled slowly down the street, carrying a placard, which read "Exempted by the Strike Committee." An occasional laundry wagon or private car appeared, and there was a clatter of hoofs on the red brick streets as a few far sighted commuters rode home on horseback. Heavily armed policemen stood at the street corners, passing jokes with people they knew. Labor guards, wearing armbands . . . patrolled the industrial district; whenever a crowd gathered, they asked the members to "break it up, fellows" or mentioned that it was a fine day to be home planting potatoes. Late in the afternoon the streets were almost deserted.[87]

The international AFL officers, who strongly opposed the general strike because it broke union contracts, began sending telegrams and arriving in Seattle to break the strike. Mayor Ole Hanson hired hundreds of temporary policemen, many recruited from fraternities at the University of

Washington, and requested National Guard assistance. In response, the attorney general and Henry Suzzallo, head of the State Defense Council, acting in place of a seriously ill Governor Ernest Lister, called in the army's First Infantry Division to Seattle. They also sent troops to Tacoma because unions there had planned sympathy strikes.[88]

Despite the fear of violent incidents, however, none occurred. In fact, the arrest records during the general strike were much lower than usual. The police docket of about one hundred cases a day dropped during the general strike to about thirty. The SCLC *Strike Bulletin* proclaimed: "Perfect order prevailed in every section of the city. This record is the result of the native instincts of the strikers and not because of any show of armed force. . . . This is our city, our state, and our nation. We are as much interested in its fair name as is any other group in the community. . . . If disorder should occur, you may be sure the strikers and their friends are not the cause of it. . . . THE WORKERS CAN ONLY WIN THROUGH ORDER. They will not permit themselves to be tricked into a show of force."[89]

According to the General Strike Committee, some twenty thousand people were fed the first day of the strike. After resolving initial problems, the committee claimed that provisions for at least forty thousand people would be provided the second day. The public could obtain meals at the following locations: the Longshoremen's Hall, the Labor Temple, the basement of the Postal and Telegraph building, the Cook's hall, Zero pool hall, the Old Masonic Temple, the City Grill, and the Swedish Club, among other locations.[90] The organizing for the strike had been effective. Mistakes were corrected, and no one went without necessary services, including food, light, heat, telephones, hospital care, public safety, and milk for children and others who needed it. Order was maintained. Labor was proud of its demonstration of solidarity and managerial competence.

By the second day of the strike, Friday, the portents of disaster had not materialized and the public was not so apprehensive. Life was orderly, basic services were being provided, and there was no violence or lawlessness. Morgan has argued that Mayor Hanson recognized the implications of this by the second day: "He must have understood something the strikers had not even admitted to themselves: that the general strike was not a means to an end but an end in itself."[91] If labor wasn't going to seize property or control of the city, if the strike was to gain concessions, the employers could wait them out. Hanson issued a proclamation assuring the public that he had things under control and that all people violating the laws would be prosecuted.

Strong remembered how Hanson had taken some of the labor leaders to lunch before the general strike. He was "amicable." He went to the office of the *Seattle Union Record* to "cajole" them—in the beginning. He was a "weather-cock in the wind . . . [but when] Ole turned against us on the second day of the general strike, we should have guessed that he had discovered our weakness." Strong identified that weakness as the lack of revolutionary intent: "We were all red in the ranks and yellow as leaders. . . . We loved the emotion of a better world coming, but all of our leaders and not a few of our rank and file had a lot to lose in the old world. The general strike put into our hands the organized life of the city—all except for guns. We could last only until they started shooting; we were one gigantic bluff. That expert in bluffing, Ole Hanson, saw this on the second day of the struggle."[92]

Hanson called the SCLC and asked the Committee of Fifteen to come to his office. Committee representatives went, but there was no progress. They agreed to meet later that day with the citizens committee, which was chaired by the president of the Chamber of Commerce. Influential businessmen argued against any type of negotiations with labor until it had purged itself of radicals.[93] Further negotiations were to be continued at a meeting later that evening. But when they gathered a third time, the citizens committee had changed its position and wanted to end negotiations with "revolutionists." There is evidence that the citizens committee knew the general strike was not revolutionary, but the open-shop proponents within the chamber had "taken their cue from Piez and decided to break the union."[94]

That same evening Hanson took steps to regain control over municipal management. He sent a message to the Committee of Fifteen stating: "I hereby notify you that unless the sympathy strike is called off by 8:00 o'clock tomorrow morning, February 8, 1919, I will take advantage of the protection offered this city by the national government and operate all essential services."[95] The committee refused. Some strikers became more determined to show that labor would not be intimidated. William Short, president of the WSFL, later recounted that Hanson's tactic of making "bombastic and flamboyant" proclamations resulted in "continuing the strike for at least three days after it would have logically and naturally been brought to an end."[96] Throughout the general strike Hanson placed stories in newspapers throughout the country characterizing the general strike as a "Bolshevik uprising" and describing how he was suppressing it.

On the morning of the third day, Saturday, a few streetcar drivers began returning to work. Some other workers had returned to jobs at restaurants and shops. The *Seattle Union Record* also began printing again. In retrospect, the General Strike Committee considered it a mistake to have stopped publication during the strike. Other newspapers, like the *Seattle Star*, put out special editions, so the only news that the public was receiving contained vitriolic attacks on labor. The strike committee did issue strike bulletins, but with minimal distribution.

During the course of the general strike the tensions among the progressives and radical factions increased. James Duncan and other progressives continually tried to get resolutions passed that would limit the duration of the strike, while the radicals within the rank and file wanted to keep it going. By the evening of the third day the Committee of Fifteen presented a resolution to the General Strike Committee stating that the strike had accomplished its goals and should be called off at midnight that night. After lengthy debate "the radicals on the GSC [General Strike Committee] convinced others that this is what class war is all about," and the committee voted the resolution down.[97]

The fourth day was a Sunday, not a working day for most people. A number of locals met to vote on whether to continue the strike, with only the longshoremen and cooks voting to keep it going. Hulet Wells presented a proposal at an SCLC meeting to suspend the general strike. This proposal was loudly cheered but eventually voted down by metal trades delegates. On this day the police raided the office of the Socialist Party and made several arrests.

By Monday, February 10, the dynamics of the general strike had changed, signaling its demise. Members of the General Strike Committee went out to talk to the rank and file; most were not enthusiastic about continuing the strike. The Teamsters had returned to work, as had others. International AFL officers had ordered many of the unions back to work. After the general strike was over, the AFL Executive Council issued this statement: "The general strike inaugurated by the SCLC was an undertaking in violation of the rules and regulations of the American Federation of Labor. The greater number of the local unions did not have the approval or sanction of their international unions and did not have their moral or financial support. Born in a spirit of insubordination, disregardful of all rules and regulations adopted by trade unions for orderly procedure . . . the strike was from its inception destined to die an early death."[98] The AFL Executive Council declared that ending the general strike was a result of their efforts, not those of the mayor or the military. The History Committee of the General Strike Committee agreed with this assessment.

Historian Murray Morgan has made an insightful observation about why enthusiasm for the general strike waned: its success, its orderliness, eventually worked against it. "The town was so quiet," Morgan wrote, "there was so little activity, that the strikers lost their feeling of unity."[99] The communications networks, the spirited mass meetings, the repressive state actions that fueled polarization had stopped. Solidarity dissipates in such an atmosphere.

By Monday the General Strike Committee accepted a resolution from the Committee of Fifteen to end the general strike on Tuesday at noon. Unions that had returned to work were asked to go out again so that all unionists could return together. If developments made it necessary for the general strike to continue, further action would be referred to the rank and file. Some of the unions, citing various constraints, did not return and go out again, while others did. By Tuesday afternoon, February 11, the "revolution" was over.

POSTSTRIKE DEVELOPMENTS

The Seattle general strike erupted during a time when labor experienced increased resources, social instability, a flourishing workplace-democracy political culture, and the zeitgeist of building a new world. The narratives of workplace-democracy activists were justified through the moral beliefs that labor creates wealth and that control over one's labor was a measure of equality and independence. Yet formidable political, economic, and cultural forces confronted the moral exuberance of Seattle labor. Changing economic conditions, state actors, and a postwar hyperpatriotism sanctioned state and vigilante repression of "radicals," which contributed to the demise of the IWW in the Pacific Northwest.

After the general strike most of the newspapers lauded Mayor Hanson and Police Chief Joel Warren as heroes who had saved Seattle from ruin. The account of Hanson as the man who stopped the "revolution" was written up in several national magazines. He resigned as mayor, toured the country giving lectures on how to stop Bolshevik revolutions, and wrote a book titled *Americanism versus Bolshevism*. It was Hanson's hope to obtain the Republican nomination for president, but Warren Harding was selected instead. Hanson thereafter packed up and moved to California.

Yet despite external repression and internal problems, the SCLC maintained a righteous anger anchored within the moral certitude of workplace-democracy culture. After the strike the *Seattle Star* and *Business Chronicle* characterized the general strike as a tragic mistake. Editorials called for labor to "clean house" and eliminate the "radicals," "anarchists," and "Bolsheviks" among labor. To this the SCLC responded: "We hasten to assure the draft slacking publisher of the *Star*, all the employers who hate labor, and all those who love to lick their boots, that we know exactly what they mean by 'reds,' we know exactly what they mean by 'bolsheviki,' exactly what they mean by 'cleaning house'; that organized labor in Seattle was never so proud of itself, that it appreciates the reds more for the enemies they have made, that it has no intention of pleasing its opponents, and that the general strike is permanently in the arsenal of labor's peaceful weapons."[100]

The attorney general's office investigated the use in Seattle of this "peaceful weapon," which they characterized as an "attempted revolution." Clarence L. Reames, assistant to the U.S. attorney general, promised prosecution of those responsible. The Department of Labor announced that proceedings would begin to deport all "unnaturalized aliens" who advocated the overthrow of the government. By February 21, Secretary of Labor William B. Wilson was making statements to the newspapers that the Seattle general strike was instituted by the "Bolsheviki" and the IWW for the sole purpose of forcing a nationwide industrial revolution in the United States.

On February 14 the IWW office was raided with thirty-nine arrests because Police Chief Warren was "tired of reading their revolutionary circulars and decided to just lock them up."[101] Based on the antisyndicalism bill, twenty-seven IWW members were charged with leading the strike. All but three were eventually released. Despite this political repression, union strikes continued and new cooperatives sprang up in the first year after the general strike. Union locals from other parts of the country requested copies of the account of what happened in Seattle from the History Committee of the General Strike Committee. The general strike had demonstrated union organization, management skills, and massive labor solidarity that became part of the historical memory of labor in the Northwest.

But the inclusion of African Americans within Seattle unions still did not move from rhetoric to practice. Shortly after the general strike a committee representing "colored workers" spoke before the SCLC. They complained of discrimination in the city's unions and asked the council to remove all barriers to their becoming union members. The request was reviewed by the Resolutions Committee, which recommended that "all locals be urged to take such steps as are necessary . . . [to provide] the same freedom for white and colored persons." The council agreed rhetorically but made no provision for enforcement, and discrimination continued among numerous locals.[102]

Piez of the Emergency Fleet Corporation acted on his threat and suspended all construction on ships built in the Seattle shipyards. He was intent on not having the yards reopen unless the unions accepted the original Macy Board decision's wage scale. The shipyard strike continued through March 17, but by April the contracts for the construction of twenty-five ships had been canceled. The loss of jobs over the next few years was dramatic. Census data indicate that the number of workers employed in manufacturing dropped from 40,853 in 1919 to 13,699 in 1921, a decrease of 66 percent, as compared with the average decrease of 23 percent in sixty-eight surveyed localities.[103]

As the loss of jobs increased, many workers blamed the general strike for the cancellation of contracts and the depression. But this obscures the fact of the inability of industry, in this case the shipyards, to convert to peacetime production. This inability was being demonstrated throughout the country. Employment statistics for the metal trades, machine products, and shipbuilding industries dropped more than 39 percent. Union membership dropped nationwide, with 60 percent of the decline in the metal trades, transportation, and shipbuilding industries.[104] Yet some unionists argued that the shipyards were being closed to intentionally break the unions.[105] Certainly the passage of the Anti-syndicalism Act in Washington State in 1919 and postwar hyperpatriotism gave license for increased state repression of workplace democracyists.

The loss of jobs and union members brought about change in the composition of the labor factions in Seattle. The closing of the shipyards and subsequent local depression caused many workers to leave Seattle in search of work, resulting in a reduction of progressive and radical activists. Writer and editor Strong described what happened: "We knew that the economic crisis of 1920–21 came to us a year before it came to others. And that our shipyard workers drifted to other cities to look for work. The young, the daring, the best fighters went. . . . So the composition of our labor movement changed. The life died out of a dozen 'workers' enterprises' which were part of our 'inevitable road to socialism.' Overexpanded cooperatives went bankrupt in a storm of recriminations. Business firms that had courted the *Union Record* with advertisements to capture the workers' trade now sensed our weakness and pressed for control of our columns. Workers fought each other for jobs and not the capitalists for power."[106]

Economic losses, state repression, and the changes in the density and composition of the labor force resulted in the demise of the once vibrant workplace-democracy political culture, which had carried the legacy of the movement for the self-governing workshop into the twentieth century. The power of the moderates increased in the following years, and this political faction became dominant among Seattle labor.

3 "TO ORGANIZE AND CONTROL THE JOB"

The San Francisco General Strike, 1934

THIS CONTROVERSY GOES FURTHER THAN JUST THE LONGSHOREMEN.
It is the intrinsic right as well as the acquired right of every American
worker to organize and control the job. The longshoremen are fighting
labor's battle and not fighting for themselves alone. They are in the grip
of a great struggle for human rights, human betterment and social
advancement.

—*Ivan F. Cox, Secretary of Local 38-79, 1934*

There is no single blueprint for a general strike. The differences
between Seattle's and San Francisco's strikes were considerable.
The San Francisco general strike grew out of a coastwide maritime strike that included riots in San Francisco and other port cities. It
occurred during the worst economic depression in U.S. history, which
was accompanied by increasing degradation of already bad working conditions. At the port of San Francisco a labor faction mobilized the rank
and file to challenge these conditions through workplace-democracy
demands—recognition of a new rank-and-file-controlled union with
worker control of the hiring hall as well as coastwide industrial organization that was inclusive of the unskilled, all races, and other nationali-
ties. Although vocabularies had been reconstructed in response to
industrial conditions, continuities with the goals and strategies of the
movement for the self-governing workshop were expressed through the
impact of the Industrial Workers of the World (IWW) and other left political orientations within West Coast maritime culture.

This chapter looks at the economic, political, and historically contingent conditions out of which the San Francisco general strike emerged. Like chapter two it identifies the distinctive cultural lenses that mediated the goals, strategies, and modes of organization proposed by labor factions, but it focuses on workplace-democracy, communist, and moderate craft union orientations—an understanding that allows us to assess cultural impact in chapter four.[1] This chapter begins with the cultural diffusion of workplace-democracy vocabularies and practices through occupational networks from the Pacific Northwest to West Coast ports including San Francisco.[2] Then I explore the demise of the International Longshoremen's Association (ILA) in San Francisco after World War I as well as the changes that took place on the docks during the Great Depression, both of which set the stage for collective action. Next the chapter focuses on the precipitating maritime and general strikes. A brief discussion of poststrike developments concludes the chapter.

DIFFUSION FROM THE PACIFIC NORTHWEST
TO SAN FRANCISCO

Since cultural forms are material, then like all things created by human beings, they are dependent on available resources and technologies, including modes of transportation, for their production and communication. This concept helps us to understand the diffusion of workplace-democracy narratives, strategies, and practices through social and occupational networks among Pacific Northwest loggers with West Coast longshoremen and seamen at the port of San Francisco. Numerous workers moved from jobs as loggers to West Coast ports in the early twentieth century. Sociologist Howard Kimeldorf has explained: "In the early days of the lumber industry, trees felled by loggers were floated downstream to the docks where longshoremen loaded them aboard steam schooners for seamen to lash in place on the deck. With this vertical integration, occupational boundaries became very fluid; many men actually followed the movement of logs from forest to dock to ship and back again. . . . Constant shuffling and reshuffling of work crews, whether aboard ship or in logging camps, generated a dense network of social contacts, exposing both factions to a correspondingly wide range of ideas. This was especially true of seamen, arguably the most cosmopolitan body of workers in the world."[3]

Oregon provided additional occupational networks for cultural diffusion through the state's two major industries—timber and agriculture. The IWW was active in logging and there was interchange among loggers and longshoremen. The state also drew agricultural workers from the Midwest, who brought Populist Party narratives and practices with them from these occupations to the docks.[4] Maritime worker Matt Meehan was formerly involved with the IWW and later became a longshoreman in Portland, Oregon. He traveled from port to port to mobilize workers during the 1934 coastwide maritime strike. Throughout these mobilizations Meehan called on the narratives of "industrial unionism" and "anticentralized authority" to mobilize workers: "In order to be successful, the maritime industry had to organize industry wide. Not necessarily under one head, they could maintain their own identity, have their officers, and so on, run their own business . . . the unions could maintain their own autonomy and so forth . . . but they had to belong to a central organization. . . . I won't say I originated the thing—'An injury to One is an Injury to All.' Well, between us it came out. . . . So I said 'This I know the old-timers will buy.' So we decided to do this program that when one local strikes, all the locals strike and we have the same demands. We'd go out the same day and go back the same day, all the contracts would be the same."[5]

In addition, there was occupational diffusion among the Australian Seamen's Unions with American ones, which contributed yet another source of workplace-democracy culture among West Coast sailors and maritime workers in San Francisco. There was significant overlap in the membership books of West Coast and Australian unions. By the 1930s the Australian seamen had adopted principles and tactics of the American IWW, but they did not have large numbers who were members.[6] In fact, San Francisco general strike leader Harry Bridges was from Australia and had been a member of the IWW for a short time in the 1920s. He quit due to the organization's refusal to sign agreements or to arbitrate.

THE GREAT DEPRESSION AND THE WATERFRONT WORKER

As in Seattle, workers at the port of San Francisco were able to negotiate generous contracts because of the increased demand for war materials during World War I. Conditions were also favorable at the San Francisco port due to the opening of the Panama Canal. Profits were high for the shipowners, who often conceded to union demands to ensure unimpeded production during the war. Prices in San Francisco rose following the armistice. The Riggers and Stevedores union in San Francisco went on strike for higher wages. In response, employers organized a campaign to hire strikebreakers. African Americans were sought because they could be paid less, as they had fewer job opportunities and felt little sympathy for unions that excluded them. One African-American strikebreaker summed it up: "I was living in Oakland and I had a wife and ten kids, out of work, and the news came out that they had a strike on the waterfront, which the Negroes weren't allowed to work."[7]

In fact, acting as strikebreakers was one of the few opportunities African Americans had to gain entrance into occupations that were inaccessible to them because of discrimination. The Pacific Coast ILA had barred "colored" people since its founding in the mid-nineteenth century. The few African Americans who worked as longshoremen at some of the ports were in segregated work gangs, as were other ethnic groups. The employers often used racial and ethnic antagonisms to pit the gangs against each other to increase productivity.

African-American strikebreakers contributed to the loss of the San Francisco Riggers and Stevedores strike in 1919.[8] But this was not the only labor defeat after the war. The Seattle and Portland locals also lost strikes, as the Pacific Coast ILA dissolved, due in part to African-American strikebreakers. Although numerous strikes have been lost because of strikebreakers of color in U.S. history, the postwar pattern was indicative of larger changes in urban and occupational demographics. A labor shortage related to the industrial production of war materials occurred during the war. As Euro-American workers went overseas as soldiers, Northern employers actively recruited African Americans to fill industrial positions that had formerly been unavailable to them.

The strikers at the San Francisco port in 1919 were fired. Newly recruited workers had to show their "blue book," indicating membership in a "company union" that replaced the ILA. In this instance African Americans were not successful in gaining a foothold through strikebreaking. Of the roughly five hundred who were hired, few were kept on permanently. Those African-American workers who stayed were not allowed into the Blue Book union and worked as gangs for only some companies.[9]

Numerous unions were destroyed in the years after the war. By 1929 overall union membership had fallen to 3,442,600 from a wartime high of 5,047,800.[10] Throughout the 1920s longshoremen competed with each other on the docks each morning to be selected for work. Whenever people are in dependent relationships, there is the potential for abuse. This method of hiring, called the "shape-up," involved considerable corruption on the part of gang bosses who hired from crowds of desperate people. Most longshoremen did not like the shape-up but they, like other workers, were afraid of losing jobs if they challenged working conditions. This sentiment is evident in the steady decline in the number of U.S. strikes from 1924 through 1929.[11]

Yet the economic busts that accompany the booms of capitalist economics were on the horizon. On October 21, 1929, the New York stock market lost two billion dollars. By January 1930 the number of unemployed had increased from 492,000 to 4,065,000.[12] The number of employed longshoremen decreased to 74,000 in 1930, from a peak figure of 86,000 in 1920.[13] Still, President Herbert Hoover was largely in denial that there actually was a depression; he felt it was merely an isolated economic downturn. For the first few years of the depression the media didn't cover it as one. Politician Franklin Roosevelt thought otherwise, however, and was elected president in 1932.

Roosevelt quickly passed the National Industrial Recovery Act (NIRA), which provided legal support for unionization. Section 7a of the NIRA, which became law in June 1933, stated that labor had a right to collectively bargain through unions of its choice. This was an invitation to challenge company unions and demand recognition of new ones controlled by employees. The number of strikes increased nationally; many were for union recognition. By 1934 there were 1,856 work stoppages carried out by roughly 1,470,000 workers.[14]

Aside from the maritime strikes (which I discuss below), three other turbulent strikes caught the public's attention—truck drivers in Minneapolis, Minnesota; auto-part workers in Toledo, Ohio; and textile workers in New England and the South. Confrontations were so intense in Toledo and Minneapolis that the governors called out the National Guard. Unions carried out these labor struggles separately, with no direct networking among activists. By and large, what the labor activists knew was what they read in the newspapers about the events.[15]

Working conditions were already bad, and the depression made them worse. To increase production, longshoremen were subjected to a "speed-up" to cover lost profits. People were fired or laid off and not replaced; their work was covered by those "lucky" enough to keep their jobs. In this exploitative environment safety rules meant little. One long-shoreman described his experiences on the docks in the early 1930s as such: "Now the winch driver is not supposed to hang a load over the men working in the square of the hatch, well, just listen to that man [the walking boss] holler 'COME IN WITH IT' while there are two loads landed in one section and the men are flooring off. Safety rules don't mean anything if he can cheat the men out of a half hour's pay. I wonder how he would like to work and have a load (very seldom less than two ton [*sic*]) hanging over his head. [He] hollers and shouts and makes the men very uneasy. . . . I believe the man gets a sadistic pleasure out of the men's discomfort. I think he really enjoys to see the men running forward and back and don't know where they are going [*sic*]."[16]

The Blue Book had been a "closed-shop" company union. Anyone who tried to organize a competing labor-controlled union was blacklisted. Yet changing state policies only partly explain collective action at the San Francisco port. The NIRA contributed to struggles for union recognition, but it was not the only cause. Mike Quinn, a writer for the long-shoremen who participated in the general strike, cautioned: "The men were at the end of their patience and would have organized the new union regardless. . . . It is more nearly correct to say that both the NRA and the organizational revolt of the longshoremen sprang from the same social causes, occurred simultaneously, and influenced each other."[17]

In December 1932 a newsletter called the *Waterfront Worker* began publication. The first issue was printed in the rented room of a Marine Workers Industrial Union (MWIU) member, although the Albion Hall group produced it. The Albion Hall labor faction, named after their meeting-place in San Francisco's Mission District, consisted of a small number of syndicalist-oriented rank-and-file longshoremen and a few Communist Party (CP) members. Although the longshoremen may have been at the end of their patience, they lacked direction and "the paper gave one."[18] The newsletter, written anonymously by "Rank and File stevedores," was circulated from person to person on the docks. It criticized working conditions, corrupt American Federation of Labor (AFL) officials or "buro-crats," and argued for the formation of a new union run by the "rank & file."

As support for organizing a new ILA union grew, three factions competed for control of it. The first was a Catholic bloc led by Lee J. Holman that supported the moderate policies of AFL officials and its members. William Lewis and Fred West led the second faction. Lewis was left on economic issues but moderate on political ones, while West was a district organizer for the Proletarian Party, a group that fell somewhere on the political spectrum between the Communist Party and the Socialist Labor Party.[19] The third was the Albion Hall faction.

During the depression the CP increased membership and was active in San Francisco. The party concentrated on distributing its newsletter, the *Western Worker*, and organizing numerous forums, meetings, demonstrations, and classes. Labor schools, like the one advertised in the *Waterfront Worker*, offered night classes on Marxian economics, principles of communism, and the history of the American labor movement. The school was organized because "all workers should know the causes of the general economic breakdown, with the wage cuts taking place."[20]

The communist MWIU tried to organize on the docks in 1931, but it was ineffective. Organizer Harry Bridges believed that the MWIU "didn't catch on at all because . . . their program was pretty revolutionary, pretty idealistic . . . despite the fact that the people felt pretty desperate, they didn't cotton too much to their . . . political views."[21] This was in contrast to the rhetoric of syndicalist-oriented longshoremen, like Bridges, in the Albion Hall faction. They communicated workplace-democracy narratives of rank-and-file control, reliance on themselves rather than on the centralized authority of AFL officials or the state, the belief that labor creates wealth, and inclusive industrial unionism, which explains why the *Waterfront Worker* had greater appeal.

Although there were links between the IWW and maritime workers at several West Coast ports, the narratives of the workplace-democracy faction in San Francisco were not as easily identifiable in 1934 as artisan republican vocabularies had been in Seattle in 1919. It is necessary to look more carefully at the meaning of the principles that the terminology communicates, as I do throughout this chapter. In some instances, however, the *Waterfront Worker* sounded similar to the *Seattle Union Record*. Consider the following use of "producer" and "parasites"—terms common to labor organizations for the self-governing workshop: "The shipowners only use you when you are of use to them, you can no longer serve them, you are junked. Stick to your class—the working class. To hell with the shipowners and THE parasites who rob us of what we produce."[22]

But the CP's problems didn't end with discourses that "didn't catch on," however. Part of the problem with the CP, according to member

Sam Darcy, was that the communists didn't have one worker on the docks. Because they were on the "outside," the creation of the Albion Hall group and the publication of the *Waterfront Worker* with rank-and-file longshoremen gave them access to maritime workers. This was at a time when the CP's strategy was to oppose the AFL's bourgeois unionism through the creation of competing unions. The goal of the CP unions was to foster a proletarian outlook that would move the members toward the eventual revolutionary overthrow of the state. At this historical moment the participation of CP members in the new ILA union actually went against party policy. The decision of some CP members to work within the Albion Hall group was made because of its momentum. Hundreds of longshoremen had signed up with the Holman-led faction, which had obtained the charter; coastwide, thousands would leave the Blue Book to join the new ILA union.

According to Darcy, CP members had to make compromises in order to work with rank-and-file longshoremen:

> In the group which published the *Waterfront Worker*, were included a minority of Communists, and other militant elements. The guiding line for this group was above all to develop a militant group of workers united with the objective of breaking the Blue Book union and to establish a real union. At times there was criticism that the *Waterfront Worker* did not take a clearly enough militant stand on this policy or that policy. When this criticism was justified, it could in every instance be traced to the desire of the Communist elements in the group not to sacrifice the unity of the militant elements for a clearer formulation on the minor questions. In other words, the group felt it was more important to attain the larger objective of developing a united militant group (not limited to Communists alone) than to refuse to make concessions to this or that backward idea amongst the workers.[23]

This quotation illustrates that despite some common interests, there were clear differences of strategies and goals among CP members in contrast to other "militant elements," meaning rank-and-file workplace-democracy organizers.

Another reason for the tactical congruence among the syndicalist-oriented maritime workers was the large number of West Coast CP members who had formerly been involved with the IWW. During the founding of the communist MWIU in 1930, more than half of the new members were former Wobblies, who had left the IWW because of its ineffectiveness.[24] Although there was strategic overlap, there were also clear distinctions between the narratives and practices of CP members and those of syndicalist-oriented rank-and-file longshoremen. Maritime workers exhibited a long history of resistance to taking orders from centralized authority, be the authorities bureaucratic CP members or East Coast AFL officials. One waterfront story tells how several longshoremen hung a CP member out of the window by his toes because he tried to impose party policy. Whether this actually happened, it communicates a message—maritime workers did not like taking orders from centralized authority.[25] Close associates to Bridges observed that "Harry never took directions from anyone."[26] This West Coast proclivity for local rank-and-file control fostered challenges to centralized authority in the union or in the state and is a distinguishing characteristic of the workplace-democracy lineage.

THE PRELUDE: THE COASTWIDE MARITIME STRIKE

Within a few weeks of the passage of the NIRA, Lee Holman was on the waterfront with petitions to abolish the Blue Book union and to encourage longshoremen to join the new ILA. The ethos was apparent in the call to organize as a single coastwide, industrial unit. At this juncture we see direct competition among political factions at the San Francisco port. Depending on who gained leadership, the goals, strategy, and understandings of what is and is not a resource would differ. One of Albion Hall's first strategic actions was to use the *Waterfront Worker* to call a meeting of new members to elect rank-and-file leadership. The Holman faction sought to remain in leadership by not having elections.[27] Holman proposed that workers wait for developments in Washington, D.C., and accept federal arbitration of disputes. In contrast, the Albion Hall faction argued that workers could not rely on Washington, and if changes were to be made, they could only be made through direct action.

The Albion Hall group proposed that the union should have a policy of regular meetings in which grievances could be aired and officers would be responsible for accounting for finances—ideas unappealing to most AFL officials and also opposed by the Holman faction. The Albion Hall faction also mobilized workers through engaging in direct action on the docks. Understanding grievances because they themselves worked under the same conditions, this faction led actions against the speed-up by slowing work time at the winches (the hoisting machine that lifts cargo) and in the hold (where the cargo is stored on the ship). Through such strategies they succeeded in enhancing the union's appeal and in recruiting new members.

Employers predictably blacklisted anyone who joined. In September 1934 four ILA members were not hired on docks where they had previously worked. When these workers went to Holman, they were told not to make trouble and advised to take individual action. But the Albion Hall faction argued for direct action over reliance on the state. At the next meeting of the local, Bridges proposed that the union strike to get the four unionists back on the job. The idea was voted down. The *Waterfront Worker* then put out a special issue calling for rank-and-file support of a strike. Bridges and others went to the docks and personally talked workers into a walkout to support the fired unionists, resulting in a strike of roughly a hundred and fifty longshoremen. The Albion Hall group responded quickly to problems on the docks through the *Waterfront Worker*, which effectively communicated their perspective and mobilized responses as noted earlier.[28] The fired longshoremen went to the Regional Labor Board using section 7a of the NIRA as the basis for their appeal, and the board ordered Matson Navigation to reinstate the workers. Soon after, most of the longshoremen along the Pacific Coast signed up in the new ILA, which the employers still refused to recognize or negotiate with, claiming that they were bound by agreements with the Blue Book union.

The Roosevelt administration had a difficult time getting employers to comply with the new NIRA policy. There were efforts to create a code that would guarantee specific wages and conditions of work for the longshoremen. During negotiations ILA president Joseph Ryan did not represent the interests of West Coast longshoremen in Washington.[29] In light of this the *Waterfront Worker* promoted a rank-and-file convention that would organize the longshoremen along the coast for direct action:

> For nine months, the men have been promised better working conditions under the NRA code, have been patiently awaiting the code to come. The shipowners have been stirred to feverish activity, preparing for trouble. . . .
>
> Another angle of the shipowners is the recent attempt to recruit negroes into the B.B. [Blue Book union] also the hiring of college boys on various docks

and the most infamous of all is the use of stool pigeons in the ranks of the ILA (one of these rats was just exposed thru the efforts of the *Waterfront Worker*). . . .

The stevedores on the Coast have only one course to follow and that is to UNITE THE COAST FOR CONCERTED ACTION, in preparation for the coming struggles. We have seen the maneuvers of the district officials to head off the Rank and File Convention. But these maneuvers are being spiked because the membership are fast awakening to the facts, that the rank and file must take a more active part in the affairs of the union if they are not to be SOLD OUT.[30]

The delegates of the rank-and-file convention (or the Pacific Coast District convention) represented fourteen thousand longshoremen elected by their coworkers from various West Coast ports. Both employers and AFL officials argued that a convention should be postponed until a new shipping code was written, but the Albion Hall faction continued to mobilize for direct action. The ethos of rank-and-file control was so strong that a motion passed to deny AFL officers status as delegates at the conference, although they could attend.

At the convention there was tension between the Holman faction, which argued in favor of waiting for a new shipping code, and the workplace-democracy faction, which was ready for direct action. The ILA officials cautioned that in the long run the longshoremen would be better off to wait for the establishment of a shipping code for the maritime industries. Section 7b of the NIRA had authorized industries to prepare operational codes to help to stimulate the economy and mitigate the economic distress of working people. Bridges and the workplace-democracy faction continued to push for direct action. He laid out their position: "Plan to wait for a code and our future as a result of the settlement of that issue: that is the conservative policy, and I for one don't agree with that and have not for some time past. . . . That is why they class me under the radical element. I have never denied it. I am used to those things. . . . I want to bring this out forcibly, we shouldn't take any notice of what the shipowners think or say about us. They would shoot us if they had the chance or could get away with it without being discovered. We are putting them on the block and we should keep them there."[31]

At the rank-and-file convention the Holman faction got its people elected to the Executive Board of the new union, but the Albion Hall faction succeeded in pushing through a number of proposals that were adopted. These included calling for coastwide contracts, a union-controlled hiring hall, pay raises, a thirty-hour week, the formation of a waterfront federation, unemployment insurance, and a resolution against ships flying the Nazi flag.[32] This last resolution was in keeping with the commitment to social issues, beyond bread-and-butter concerns, of the "reform labor" trajectory and workplace-democracy traditions.

The convention elected a delegation to present their demands to the employers,[33] but the employers refused to negotiate, called the delegation members "communists," and insisted on speaking with union officials. When convention attendees heard this, they proposed a coastwide strike if their demands were not met by March 23. Although Holman, now the president of the San Francisco local, opposed the strike, a rank-and-file vote was taken and the majority favored having one. In preparation a strike committee of twenty-five rank-and-file members was elected. The strike had three primary goals: (1) to achieve recognition of the Pacific Coast District ILA, which would mean signing a coastwide contract; (2) to gain higher wages; and (3) to establish union-controlled hiring halls.[34]

The regional labor director of California, George Creel, told the employers that they should enter into negotiations with the union, and negotiations thus began. The employers rejected the demands of the convention. They equated a union-controlled hiring hall with a closed shop and argued that it was in violation of section 7a of the NIRA, which stated that there should be no discrimination against employees, union or nonunion. They also were unwilling to discuss changing the shape-up method of hiring or to make concessions, figuring that it would be worth investing several million dollars in the short run if they could destroy the union in the long run.[35]

As the strike approached, it became clear to the Albion Hall faction that Holman would undermine it if he remained in a leadership position. He had written ILA president Joseph Ryan in New York to say that he opposed the strike and that it was being forced on the union by a radical minority.[36] Ryan's political outlook was representative of the moderate craft union orientation and shared the most similarities with the Holman faction within the ILA. The East Coast ILA was organized on a craft basis, and strikes were used as a last resort. Rather than direct action,

Ryan relied heavily on patronage relations and formal and informal negotiations with employers and state actors to achieve concessions. He had publicly supported the shape-up method of hiring, in stark contrast to the Albion Hall faction.

Bridges proposed a solution that drew on the cultural resonance for rank-and-file control. He proposed that workers at each dock in San Francisco and Oakland elect a member to a strike committee. Those who worked regularly in gangs but not at a particular dock would elect three members, and those who worked as "casual" laborers and were hired in the daily shape-up would elect six members. The committee would then have roughly fifty representatives. Bridges was elected chairman of the strike committee.[37]

Informed that there was to be a coastwide strike on the West Coast, Roosevelt sent a wire asking for a delay and appointed a committee to investigate the situation. The strike was postponed. During the board hearings held in late March, the ILA officials had been flexible on the issue of the union-controlled hiring, which disregarded and disrespected rank-and-file priorities. In early April the board recommended "representation elections for longshoremen under supervision of the Regional Labor Board's hiring halls in each port as a 'joint venture for the employers and the longshoremen' with methods of dispatching men to be determined locally; wages and hours to be fixed by an arbitration board consisting of an impartial chairman, nine employer and nine employee members (three on each side from each of the coast states)."[38] The employers responded with an offer to recognize the ILA along with other unions (meaning the Blue Book company union) and agreed to a dispatching hall jointly controlled, but they made no mention of wages or hours. The ILA district representative accepted the offer. When the details of this agreement were provided to the rank and file, Bridges objected and confronted the district representative.

Sick of ineffectual negotiations, Local 38-79 suspended Holman as president. The new ILA union voted to strike on May 9, 1934. Senator Robert F. Wagner, chairman of the National Labor Board (NLB), sent telegrams requesting that workers call off the proposed strike and allow the board to reconsider the matter. Despite this, on May 9 roughly twelve hundred longshoremen went on strike along the Pacific Coast from San Diego to the Canadian border.[39] Ryan wired the Pacific Coast secretary of the ILA, J. C. Bjorkland, and suggested modifications of union demands. From Ryan's perspective, representative of a moderate craft orientation, higher wages and better working conditions should solve the problem. He sent a counterproposal suggesting an increase in hourly wages and overtime. Bjorkland's reply indicated that the concerns of the West Coast longshoremen went beyond bread-and-butter issues, stating: "Ryan's wire premature. No cognizance taken of other vital factors at issue. Wages and hours not only consideration."[40]

On May 13, San Francisco's most powerful union, the Teamsters, voted unanimously not to transport merchandise to and from the docks. Michael Casey, the moderate AFL president of the Teamsters Union, tried to block this action but was unsuccessful. His concern was that Teamster contracts discouraged sympathetic strikes.[41] Strike momentum continued to increase as the seamen and marine firemen voted to strike. When the maritime workers united and struck the coast, they initiated the first coastwide, industrywide strike in American history. This sequence of events so alarmed state officials that the governors of California, Oregon, and Washington sent appeals for federal intervention. Assistant Secretary of Labor Edward McGrady flew to San Francisco. By May 20 the sympathy strike had spread to the Masters, Mates, and Pilots Union, whose members voted to go on strike for their own demands.

At the inception of the coastwide strike the workplace-democracy faction at the San Francisco port took the first steps toward racial inclusion. The massive strike loss after World War I had elicited concern among unions as well as within the CP. Yet the IWW had promoted racial inclusion within industrial unions early in the twentieth century, as had the Knights of Labor before them in the nineteenth century. African Americans were recruited not only to join the new ILA union, but also to occupy positions of power within it. Two African Americans served on the strike committee.[42] The workplace-democracy faction and African-American unionists did outreach on the docks. The rank-and-file strike committee also did outreach to prominent members of the African-American community. They were successful in recruiting union organizer C. L. Dellums of the Sleeping Car Porters Union to help deter strikebreaking. Dellums recounted what happened at one meeting:

> There was a white man and a Negro running the meeting. . . . They whispered and told me to sit down, that I couldn't take the floor, I couldn't speak. So I turned to the crowd and said, 'Most of you fellows know me by sight. I am

C. L. Dellums. I want to speak to you. . . . If you want to hear what I have to say, make this guy shut up and let me talk.' And so they did. . . . So I gave them a good rabble rousing. I gave them first a good educational talk on labor and civil rights where we had so much in common. Then I asked them to give me their word, and I told them, 'I know you'll keep your word with me, I always keep mine with you. Give me your word you will not break the strike, all who will stand.' And they stood almost to the man. So I said, 'OK, since we're not going to break the strike, the meeting is over. Let's get the hell out of here!'[43]

Outreach and recruitment to positions of power within the union communicated its sincerity. But the history of exclusion and suspicion among Euro- and African-American workers required additional steps to construct a class-centered collective identity.

Racial solidarity was communicated through displays, speeches, and rhetoric. Some of the workers in the seamen's unions, which had recently joined the strike, were Chinese and Filipino. One public display of the "industrial unionist" narrative took place on May 13 in San Francisco. One source recounted: "Up the thoroughfare came the 5,000 with the stars and stripes and the blue banner of the ILA in the lead. Close behind was the union leadership including Bridges, Henry Schmidt and John Shoemaker. Marching with them was a black member of the Strike Committee. Stretching down the wide boulevard, eight abreast, came the longshoremen, their wives, children and supporters, including striking cooks, Chinese seamen, Filipino seamen and members of other sympathetic unions, carrying placards proclaiming their support for the cause."[44]

The *Waterfront Worker* was a primary vehicle for the construction of class identity, which challenged the racial privileges of Euro-American unionists. The degree to which class conflict was emphasized was crucial to the success of these discourses. As the abuses of employers became the focus of opposition and as polarization increased, experiences of exploitation and repression on the docks were constructed to enhance a common class identity. The *Waterfront Worker* communicated discourses and images of a fighting (and masculinist) spirit shared by maritime workers in opposition to employers. It politicized gendered identities and the characteristics valued within working-class culture: physical strength and not letting oneself be "pushed around." This imagery, drawn on again and again in the *Waterfront Worker*, valorized the rank and file, "the boys," in opposition to both employers and union officials, who were portrayed as lazy, corrupt "slave drivers" who "feathered their nests" through the labor of the longshoremen. The only way to "clean up the docks," they believed, was through rank-and-file control, inclusive industrial organization, and direct action.

But to achieve solidarity, racial inclusion was imperative. Racial divisions were characterized as employer strategies to divide workers. A worker could be persuaded to accept African Americans in the union, not through eliminating his racism, but by pointing out that when workers divide, the employers win. This theme was communicated in editorials, letters to the editor, and cartoons. One of these showed African-American and Euro-American unionists standing side by side with the word "Solidarity" written over their heads. The political culture of maritime workers exhibited a resonance for the industrial unionist ethic, providing a cultural space for workplace-democracy organizers to promote racial solidarity and old IWW stories about how the employers win through dividing the workers. Limited strikebreaking by African Americans and skirmishes did occur during the strike, but not enough to undermine it.

The industrial unionist principle, however, did not result in the incorporation of women, who as a group constituted no threat as strikebreakers. Gender roles were traditional and patriarchal. The inclusion of women into union activities involved such symbolic gestures as including women speakers at meetings and publishing occasional letters from female relatives of longshoremen in the *Waterfront Worker*. An ILA women's auxiliary was chartered in June 1934 to do publicity and fundraising and to provide moral support to the strikers and their families. Its membership mostly consisted of the wives of longshoremen. The women's auxiliary participated in picketing during the strike but ceased when the ILA strike committee asked them to.[45]

Women were also involved in strike activities through the International Labor Defense (ILD) organization. The offices, including the one in San Francisco, were mostly organized and managed by women CP members. The organization's stated purpose was "to defend workers who are arrested, not for any crime, but for union, political, or working class organizational activity. It also opposes and fights for the repeal of all laws designed, not to suppress crime, but to enable financial interests to use the courts against labor. Its function is to provide legal defense, bail, mass campaigns, prison relief and aid to families of prisoners."[46] Financial aid took the form of a Prisoners Relief Fund that helped to support the families of imprisoned activists. The children of these families were "considered 'wards' of the organization, in some cases activists took them into their homes."[47] Assaults against organized labor and other "dissidents" escalated during the depression. One member of the San Francisco branch of the ILD, Elaine Black Yoneda, was known as the "Red Angel" because of the legal and financial aid she provided strikers. The only woman, she was considered an "honorary member" of the strike committee.

The CP provided other forms of support. To try to lessen the likelihood that the unemployed would become strikebreakers, they distributed leaflets throughout poor neighborhoods. The Unemployed Councils, many of which had been organized through the CP, not only refused to take jobs as strikebreakers, but some unemployed people even joined the strikers on the picket lines. Nevertheless, strikebreakers were recruited from various locations. Some were from distant cities, while others were college students from the University of California. Support also came from small farmers who contributed food. The farmers mostly supported the maritime workers. One longshoreman said: "We had no trouble getting donations. They knew the hardships they went through when they were sharecroppers. Their heart was always with the working people. We didn't have enough trucks to pick up all they wanted to give."[48]

But other unemployed workers were not so supportive, applying for maritime jobs. Strikebreakers were given police escorts to several vessels where they received food, lodging, and entertainment provided by their employers. The lives of longshoremen and seamen were hard, and physical endurance was a test of how well someone could handle abusive life conditions and come out on top. As is common in exclusively male occupations, bravado thrived. The skills developed through physical combat were used to defend against "scabs," who replaced the striking maritime workers.

Fights between pickets and strikebreakers occurred at all ports. In Portland strikers stormed the Council Chambers at City Hall to expose the police brutality that had been taking place on the waterfront. They threw down the bloody shirt of a striker in front of the mayor. The violence in Portland was so out of control that while Senator Wagner was touring the waterfront, police fired on his car. No one was hurt.[49] Rioting continued on May 17, as longshoremen broke through a barricade in Oakland and boarded the steamship the *Oregon Maru*. Several strikebreakers were injured. The ILD helped the arrested protestors with legal aid.[50]

The coastwide strike was having an impact as industries increasingly lacked raw materials. Thousand of tons of cargo were tied up on the docks. State and union officials attempted to mediate the strike without success. The ILA sent a letter to Roosevelt's Mediation Board, stating that for negotiations to proceed (1) all provisions were to be referred back to the general membership of all ports for a vote, and (2) no one was to go back to work until the demands of other striking unions were met.[51] By May 28, when ILA president Ryan first arrived in San Francisco from New York, negotiations had reached an impasse. Part of the problem had to do with Thomas Plant, the president of the Waterfront Employers Union (WEU), who kept insisting that he could bargain for San Francisco employers only. Yet employers associations along the coast were networking with each other to keep abreast of developments. For example, Waterfront Employers of Seattle (WES) representative Frank Foisie telephoned employers in Seattle to tell them the terms of an offer Plant made to the ILA. They approved Plant's proposal.[52]

Ryan, with the support of the moderate "business unionist" Dave Beck, leader of the Seattle Teamsters, made a backdoor agreement with the employers.[53] But district ILA officials decided to submit the proposal to a coastwide referendum. Assistant Secretary of Labor McGrady tried to mediate the dispute. He first requested negotiation with AFL officials who could bind the rank and file to agreements, but practices of rank-and-file control among West Coast maritime workers made such agreements unacceptable. Angry at the rank and file's actions, McGrady made public statements declaring that a "strong radical element within the ranks of the longshoremen seems to want no settlement of this strike."[54] The employers seized the moment, and the president of the San Francisco Chamber of Commerce quickly issued similar statements to the press. Most of the newspapers in San Francisco were biased in favor of the employers. Three supported them quite openly: the *San Francisco Examiner*, the *Call-Bulletin*, and the *San Francisco Chronicle*. William Randolf Hearst owned the first two papers, and the Dollar Steamship Company had a financial investment in Hearst Publications; the *San Francisco Chronicle* was independently owned and had heavy investment from the Fleishhacker shipping interests.[55] After realizing what had happened, McGrady tried to issue a retraction, but the employers' framing of a conflict between Americanism and "alien radicals" continued to dominate the press throughout the strike.

The president's mediation board was still trying to work out an agreement, especially over the issue of the hiring hall. The board made a proposal for government-controlled hiring halls through a committee of government, employer, and union representatives, which was rejected by both sides. In the *San Francisco Examiner*, Bridges stated that the union had rejected the proposal, yet a representative of the District Committee stated that the union had not yet made a decision. Notably, the ILA's response exhibited dual authority emerging within the union between AFL officials and the rank-and-file workplace-democracy faction.

Some of the confusion can be linked to Joseph Ryan. Decision making by bureaucratic officials was more acceptable within the politically moderate ILA on the East Coast. From the time Ryan stepped off the plane from New York, he made announcements and agreements without consulting the rank and file. Ryan initially offered to give up the closed-shop demand in exchange for union recognition. This offer was rejected by the rank and file through a statement by Bridges that put him publicly at odds with Ryan within a few days of Ryan's arrival. Targeting AFL officials, Bridges declared: "Settlement for mere recognition may mean a lot to national heads of the International Longshoremen's Association who get fat salaries. But the workers are going to hold out for nothing less than a closed shop."[56]

A challenge to the practices of the AFL hierarchy was coalescing among the workplace-democracy faction and its supporters among the rank and file. In the midst of this the president of the Board of Harbor Commissioners in Los Angeles announced that the strike was costing them roughly $60,000 a month through loss of wharf and dock charges. He added that ship arrivals had declined from 117 in the preceding week to 78. Lumber shipments had fallen from more than four million board feet to zero.[57]

A meeting was held in late May, which included Assistant Secretary of Labor McGrady, employer representatives, Ryan, and a couple of ILA officials from the Northwest, but no one from the rank-and-file strike committee. They agreed on a contract that recognized the ILA, contracted separately at ports with hiring halls staffed by union and nonunion workers without preference; wages and hours would be settled by arbitration. Those present were satisfied with the agreement and reported to the press that these negotiations were the basis for settling the strike. The next day, however, this agreement was unanimously rejected at an ILA meeting of more than three thousand rank-and-file members.[58] Dean Henry Francis Grady, the chairman of the mediation board, recommended federal legislation that would allow mediation boards to impose acceptance of "fair negotiations." But President Roosevelt responded to Grady's suggestion by referring the issue back to the mediation board for further negotiations.[59]

Police repression was stepped up on the Embarcadero piers as they began to enforce city laws against picketing. Police also attacked a Communist Youth League march. It was the league's intention to show support for the maritime strike and to speak out against fascism and war. The police broke up the march for not having a permit, however, and sent twenty-four participants to the hospital in the process.[60]

Also in late May the International Seamen's Union held a membership meeting of all crafts and passed a resolution that reaffirmed their commitment to the ILA. They agreed not to return to work until the demands of all unions had been met. Workers in foreign docks were sending messages of solidarity from ports in Canada, the Netherlands, and New Zealand. These workers assured the Pacific Coast ILA that they would refuse to unload "scab" cargo.[61]

THE GENERAL STRIKE

A meeting took place on May 21, attended by about sixty prominent business leaders who were addressed by Roger Lapham, the president of the American Hawaiian Steamship Company. They elected an action committee with seven members, who in turn opened communications with Assistant Secretary of Labor McGrady as well as representatives of shipping interests in all ports. Another meeting was held on June 1, attended by roughly fifty employers, and another on June 5, with about a hundred in attendance. At these meetings plans were laid to use the police to open the port. Later it became known that the participants had also decided to invest authority for taking action to end the strike in the Industrial Association (IA) rather than with the shipowners.[62]

Shortly thereafter the Industrial Association of San Francisco sent a telegram to President Roosevelt warning that "industrial conflict of a character too serious to contemplate" would result from their attempt to move cargo and that a solution had to be found. Roosevelt did not acknowledge or reply to this telegram. The association also sent a telegram to Secretary of Labor Frances Perkins, asking her to intervene; she, too, did not respond.[63] In retrospect, Roosevelt thought the strike was in large part the fault of business interests in San Francisco. At a press conference in September 1934, he stated "off the record" that there were two primary elements responsible for the general strike. The first consisted of "hot headed young leaders who had no experience in organized labor," and the second was made up of "the old, conservative crowd just hoping that there would be a general strike, being clever enough to know that a general strike always fails."[64]

By mid-June both the employers and the longshoremen had rejected tentative contracts, and both groups maintained their positions. Rumors began to circulate that the IA was going to "open the port" by force and that the unions would respond with a general strike. The *Waterfront Worker* urged solidarity among maritime unions and attacked the "misleaders" who were trying to undermine the strike (Figure 3). Mayor Angelo Rossi made a last effort to settle the dispute. He called Ryan back to San Francisco and they met with Plant, who represented the WEU. Once again Ryan's bureaucratic orientation precluded consulting with the rank and file about the details of a new agreement.

The new agreement differed little from the May 28 one that had been rejected by the entire West Coast rank and file. It proposed joint control of the hiring halls, a separate contract for the longshoremen without regard to the other striking maritime workers, and wages and hours to be decided through arbitration. But this agreement included two new clauses: First was a sanction against sympathy strikes. The second stated: "We guarantee the observance of this agreement by the International Longshoremen's Association membership."[65] It was signed in Rossi's office on June 16. Casey, the moderate AFL president of the Teamsters Union, committed the Teamsters to return to work even if the longshoremen didn't accept this agreement. The newspapers ran front-page stories emphasizing how this was the best contract possible and how it was going to end the strike.

The issue of control over the hiring halls was perhaps the most important. While conceding to other demands, the workplace-democracy

VOL 2 NO. 15   SAN FRANCISCO, CALIF.   JUNE 12, 1934

STICK TOGETHER! SPREAD THE STRIKE!

We are now in the fifth week of the most solidly organized rank and file strike ever witnessed on the Pacific Coast. The seamen organized in the MWIU and the rank and file ISU members worked to call all seamen out on strike. Attempts have been made to form a united front of all seamen, but the ISU officials and the police have worked hand in hand to defeat such moves. Scharrenberg tried to herd the seamen back to work for $50.00 a month but the membership was ready to throw him out of the window and the great misleader had to back down.

After the militant action of Northwest membership "do nothing Bonnet" came out with a proposal that 50 ILA members be deputized to preserve "law and order", on the waterfront, but the rank and file spiked that move immediately.

He also was responsible for the loading Alaskan ships with the necessities of life, such as cast iron pipes, bricks, and fish traps supplies.

Nigstead, the Portland president issued orders permitting the unloading of 14,000 stacks of sugar for the poor cannery owners, and the unloading of tree spray on the grounds that the bugs were running away with the trees.

In Pedro, the famous trio, Pete, Patterson, and Hull are doing everything possible to keep the rank and file from carrying on militant picketing. Their policy was to have six pickets before each dock, even going so far as to have the "Red Squad" okay the picket list.

Despite the manouvers of the misleaders, the rank and file (Continued page 2, col. 1)

FIG 3. *"Stick Together! Spread the Strike!" From the* Waterfront Worker, ILWU *Anne Rand Memorial Research Library,* ILWU *Library, San Francisco.*

faction refused to arbitrate this one. Organizing and controlling the job was an intrinsic American right, as noted in Ivan F. Cox's ILA radio address quoted at the beginning of this chapter. Not having the right to workplace control was equated with "involuntary servitude" later in that radio broadcast: "If the longshoremen submit to any other proposal other than union control of hiring halls, he surrenders his right to any job in the industry to which his labors have been the means of building up . . . through an established system of blacklisting or else be subject to involuntary servitude."[66]

Several thousand longshoremen met on June 17. At the meeting Bridges announced that if the agreement received two-thirds of the rank-and-file vote for the entire Pacific Coast, the longshoremen would go back to work. Ryan was late, and by the time he got to the meeting, the agreement had been subjected to harsh criticism. Bridges confronted Ryan about not consulting the rank and file. By this point everyone was fed up with Ryan. By unanimous vote the rank and file took the power to negotiate out of the hands of the AFL officials and elected a Joint Marine Strike Committee (JMSC), with five representatives from each striking union, to conduct negotiations. Harry Bridges was its chairperson.

All negotiations were called off when the longshoremen rejected the last agreement, as far as the employers were concerned. Always persistent (to say the least), the rank and file sent representatives from their newly formed JMSC to the mayor's office to negotiate. Some of the ILA's written demands presented to Mayor Rossi included recognizing the union, imposing no penalties on strikers, agreeing not to hire nonunion workers until the ILA supply was exhausted, and establishing a union-controlled hiring hall. If the above was agreed to, the demands regarding hours and wages could be submitted to arbitration. Finally, congruent with workplace-democracy traditions of labor autonomy, the JMSC called for committees of maritime workers from "each gang to try men for drunkenness, pilfering or shirking of work."[67]

The idea of a general strike had been promoted in the *Waterfront Worker* as early as May 1934. After the defeat of the June 16 agreement there was increased discussion of a general strike. William Dunne, writing from a communist perspective, maintained that the MWIU affiliating with the Trade Union Unity League (TUUL) first promoted the staging of such a strike. The strike committee, led by Bridges, endorsed the proposal but the San Francisco and Oakland Central Labor Councils opposed the idea.[68] By about mid-June the International Association of Machinists began sending out a "general strike call" to other unions; around the same time the ILA's women's auxiliary began distributing flyers declaring: "To the Women! . . . Forward to a General Strike" (see Figure 4). On June 20, when the machinists were voting on the general strike proposal, the Oakland Teamsters had already taken a vote on June 19. At this time the waiters, window washers, and bookbinders were preparing to take a similar vote.[69]

As part of the plans to break the strike, the IA formed a subsidiary called the Atlas Trucking Company to move the cargo through the pickets. Representatives from the IA, the Chamber of Commerce, the police chief, and the harbor commissioners met to discuss their plans to open the port. They agreed that the trucks carrying cargo would not be armed but would have full police protection and that the movement of cargo would begin by June 28.

A representative from the IA called the mayor and told him that they were ready to open the port. Rossi responded by asking for another day to let McGrady continue negotiations. At the same time he called Washington, D.C., to warn of the likelihood of future violence. On the evening of June 26, Roosevelt created the National Longshoremen's Board (NLB) through an executive order. The date for Atlas operations was pushed back a week while the NLB tried unsuccessfully to mediate the dispute.

On July 2 radio stations announced that the port would be opened that day at 3 P.M. According to the strike committee's strike bulletin, eight thousand strikers had gathered at the waterfront, and as a result the port remained closed. In contrast, newspapers reported that the mayor had requested the IA to "halt action" or that the police had lacked escorts to protect the trucks. The strike committee argued that no action was taken because the truck drivers refused to drive the cargo through after seeing the number of pickets at the docks.[70]

On July 3 the newspapers announced that the port would be opened that day. Although Police Chief William J. Quinn asked the public to stay away from the waterfront, thousands of San Francisco residents nonetheless came to watch events. At 11 A.M. the police cleared the area around Pier 38. A few hours later the pier doors opened, and eight patrol cars came out, followed by five trucks loaded with cargo.[71] Writer Mike Quinn, who directly observed the events, described what happened next:

TO THE WOMEN!

WIVES, MOTHERS, SISTERS and ALL STRIKE SYMPATHIZERS:

Our men have been on strike for six weeks, their ranks are still solid. Their determination to win is steadfast. They have out-witted the maneuvers of the shipowners. They have withstood the brutal attacks of the police. They have exposed the lying charges of the Chamber of Commerce. The strikers' ranks remain unbroken. They stand ready to face any attack from any quarter and we the women and strike sympathizers must rally to the support of these courageous fighters.

The longshoremen's and seamen's strike is the fight of all workers. They are fighting for the right to live, fighting for recognition of THEIR Union. We must all help. If they lose—we all lose.

The women's auxiliary of the I. L. A. is calling an open air meeting on the corner of

MISSION and STEUART STREETS
FRIDAY, JUNE 15, 2 P. M.

to petition Chief Quinn to permit peaceful picketing on the waterfront. We appeal to all women and strike sympathizers to attend.

FIGHT FOR OUR RIGHTS!
FORWARD TO A GENERAL STRIKE!

WOMEN'S AUXILIARY
LOCAL 38-79, I. L. A.

1171 Market Street   Phone UNderhill 5043

To the Women, ILWU Library

FIG 4. "To the Women!" From Auxiliary Local 38-79, files of the ILWU Archives in the Anne Rand Memorial Research Library, ILWU Library, San Francisco.

A deafening roar went up from the pickets . . .

With single accord the great mass of pickets surged forward. The Embarcadero
became a vast tangle of fighting men. Bricks flew and clubs battered skulls.
The police opened fire with revolvers and riot guns. Clouds of tear gas swept
the picket lines and sent the men choking in retreat. Mounted police were
dragged from their saddles and beaten to the pavement. . . . Squads of police
who looked like Martian monsters in their special helmets and gas masks led
the way. . . . The fighting continued for four hours. Finally overcome by gas,
the pickets retreated up side streets and allies, battling every inch of the way. . . .
Scattered fighting continued throughout the afternoon.[72]

This exemplifies the state "regulating" workers to maintain the private
property rights of employers. After opening the port, Police Chief Quinn
received a message from John Forbes, president of the IA, expressing
the association's gratitude.[73]

The ILA strike bulletin for July 3 argued that the port hadn't really
been opened, however, and the boxes moved didn't really contain
cargo. Rather, the bulletin stated:

They have moved a half dozen old trucks with unlicensed drivers and gun-
men. The freight they claim to be moving is empty boxes. They certainly
put on a good show—lining up the entire Police Department for the movie
cameras.

They still haven't opened the port. They have opened the hospitals, cracked
skulls—and turned DECENT HUMAN BEINGS INTO RAVING MANIACS.[74]

The trucks continued running, but on the next day, July 4, they stopped
because of the holiday. A press release in the newspapers stated that they
planned to continue the following day. The attempt to move cargo thus
began again on July 5, later known as "Bloody Thursday." The police force
had increased in size and was more heavily armed. Several hundred strikers charged a police line at the base of Rincon Hill, located close to the
pier. The strikers hurled rocks while the police attacked with tear gas
bombs, which some strikers picked up and threw back at them. Other
strikers built barricades to block the police.

Near ILA headquarters the police shot three men, two of whom died, one instantly. The other struggled to get up but couldn't; he died shortly thereafter. Strikers continued fighting the police as the theme of news stories became "blood-blood-blood."[75] By 2 P.M. the fighting subsided, only to resume within the hour when the strikers stormed down Mission Street in an attempt to gain control of the area next to the ILA head-quarters. Here the strikers outnumbered the police. The police again attacked, their bullets hitting the windows of buildings. At this point California Governor Frank Merriam declared a state of emergency in San Francisco and ordered the National Guard to the waterfront, where some were stationed by nightfall.

That afternoon Elaine Black of the ILD received a call from Henry Schmidt, one of the strike committee leaders and a member of the Albion Hall faction. Schmidt asked Black to come down to the morgue to iden-tify the body of someone who had been shot. Because she was due at a meeting at five o'clock, she was hesitant but decided to go because the corpse was wearing an ILD button. Black recalled: "When I took the sheet off it was the man I had the appointment with. . . . I said, 'No, it can't be, it can't be. I was supposed to meet him at five o'clock.' It was Nick Coundeorakis, better known as Nick Bordoise—an active ILD member, a communist. . . . I had seen people with gunshot wounds, broken limbs and split heads, but I had never really seen a cadaver . . . someone who had been murdered in the line of action . . . to find him with a bullet in his back. There was no other mark of violence on him; he was shot in the back."[76] The other man killed was Howard Sperry, a longshoreman and World War I veteran.

With the state's flagrant use of violence, and increased repression embodied in the National Guard presence, the strikers were overcome by a sense of powerlessness. The port had been opened, although it was operating inefficiently. But there was one last option. On the evening of July 6, JMSC representatives proposed a resolution for a general strike at a San Francisco Labor Council (SFLC) meeting. Alarmed, the SFLC proposed an alternative resolution for the appointment of a Strike Strategy Committee (SSC) to organize plans for all San Francisco labor. The resolution was worded in such a way as to be interpreted as forming a committee to investigate matters or a committee to organize a general strike.[77]

The SSC was appointed by Edward Vandeleur, the politically moder-ate president of the SFLC. He named himself as chairman, and the committee requested that all labor organizations freeze plans for a general strike until they had a chance to become more familiar with developments. Recognizing that they could not stop a general strike, the moderate SFLC officials intended to gain control. Through the creation of the SSC, they could usurp control from the rank-and-file JMSC and maneuver the general strike to a rapid conclusion.[78] The JMSC went directly to the rank and file the next day. They called a meeting with delegates from all of the city's unions about mobilizing for a general strike. Delegates were strongly in favor of having one, but confused about taking immediate action, given the role of the SSC.[79]

That weekend the bodies of the two dead protesters were displayed at the ILA headquarters, where thousands of men and women paid tribute. A funeral procession was held on July 9. No police were present, and ILA members were granted the authority to keep order. Thousands marched along with the trucks that carried the dead. Thousands of San Francisco residents lined the streets to watch the procession. Author Quinn recounted an episode in which several well-dressed businessmen from Montgomery Street "stood amazed and impressed." Yet they kept their hats on. Marchers shouted immediately for the businessmen to take their hats off. "The tone of voice was extraordinary," wrote Quinn. "The reaction was immediate. With quick, nervous gestures, the businessmen obeyed."[80]

Writer Paul Eliel, who sympathized with the employers, described the procession as "one of the strangest and most dramatic spectacles that had ever moved along Market Street. . . . Its dramatic qualities moved the entire community without regard to individual points as to the justice and righteousness of the strikers' cause."[81] Most participants in these events agreed that the march increased worker solidarity and public support for the strikers, which enabled a general strike to take place. The funeral march signified that the state and employers had crossed a line. They had flagrantly destroyed any semblance of state neutrality and violated deeply felt notions of justice shared by laborers across the political spectrum. After the march was over the National Guard presence was increased, and martial law was extended to include more territory.

The NLB asked that all issues be submitted for arbitration. The Waterfront Employers from San Francisco, Portland, and Los Angeles agreed to arbitrate conditions for the longshoremen but claimed that they could not do so for the seamen, as their demands and representation were unclear. The ILA made an offer to submit the question of arbitration to a rank-and-file vote. Representatives of the Seamen and the Masters, Mates and Pilots indicated that they would arbitrate some conditions but not the hiring hall or union recognition; no progress was made, however.

On July 9 the Alameda Labor Council adopted a resolution asking seventy-nine unions to take a strike vote on walking out in support of the longshoremen. With talk of a general strike becoming serious, the NLB commenced with testimonies. During hearings held on July 9, 10, and 11, Bridges presented evidence before the board that employers along the coast were well organized to break unions and that without control over the hiring hall, all was lost, as ILA union members would be blacklisted. In the midst of these developments, the WEU sent a letter to the San Francisco longshoremen arguing for the joint-controlled hiring hall proposed in the June 16 agreement, rather than one controlled by the longshoremen, a concession they refused to arbitrate.

The Teamsters gathered at an auditorium, with Bridges and other maritime strikers waiting outside. They were to vote on whether to go out on strike in support of the maritime workers. Vandeleur and other AFL officials from the SSC asked for a postponement of the strike vote for a few more days. Casey, president of the San Francisco Teamsters, also asked that no strike take place. The officials were booed, and the audience began shouting "Bridges," upon which several Teamsters brought him into the auditorium to speak. Bridges received an enthusiastic welcome.

Bridges was an extremely effective speaker in regard to the idioms of speech he used as well as the substance of his presentations. Retired seaman Revels Cayton recalled it this way: "What Harry gave to the longshoremen [was] . . . a whole philosophical approach to life. He'd go to the longshoremen meetings and get on that mike and talk a while. And he could really take a group of 2,000 men and make them think. . . . That was the thing about him. He'd explain it so well that when he got through, there was no more argument."[82] At the auditorium Bridges spoke to the Teamsters about the need for labor solidarity. When one member of the audience asked what course of action should be taken, Bridges answered that it was the decision of the rank-and-file Teamsters. They voted 1,220 to 271 to strike if the maritime workers' strike had not been settled by July 12.[83]

Later Bridges stated that when the employers tried to open the port, they "had made a foolish move . . . because when they started to put strikebreakers in the place of the Teamsters' union, which was an old established and conservative union, and they started to call the Teamsters a bunch of reds, it didn't work."[84] It was at this juncture that the maritime unions got the complete support of the Teamsters. By July 12 twenty other unions had voted in favor of a general strike, some unanimously. On this day the general strike began to unfold. Some deliveries of food, gas, and coal had been stopped. Residents started to stock up on goods, emptying the shelves of local grocery stores. Those who had the resources to leave the city did so.

Because the union officials on the SSC were subject to legal constraints, they created a General Strike Committee to handle the situation, consisting of five members from each of the cities' AFL unions. The committee met on the morning of July 14 and voted to create an executive committee of twenty-five members. Vandeleur became president, while Bridges was defeated for the position of vice president by Clyde Deal of the Ferryboatmen.[85] The new committee soon met with the JMSC. Bridges argued in favor of calling a general strike, but the committee was not persuaded. The mayor called a meeting of officials and legal advisers to determine exactly what powers he had to declare a state of emergency if a general strike took place. Governor Merriam released a statement to the press that he would declare martial law unless strikers permitted the transportation of medical supplies and food. By this point some restaurants were closed, and the police had ordered that all firearms be removed from shop windows.

The next morning the General Strike Committee issued a last statement to the press, calling for the employers to submit all questions in dispute to the NLB and to allow the longshoremen the right to have control over its union headquarters, in order to "avert" the general strike. By July 15 most of the streetcars and taxis had quit running. Armed convoys of food trucks were to be brought into the city through order of the governor. As chairman of the JMSC, Bridges, along with representatives of the Pacific Coast District, sent a letter to the NLB stating that they could not agree to take a referendum vote on arbitration until "the question of the control of hiring halls is disposed of [and] . . . A satisfactory understanding has been arrived at between the maritime unions and the shipowners."[86]

The electrical and typographical unions decided not to join the strike on Sunday; thus light, power, and newspapers continued service. The mayors of six East Bay communities issued a joint proclamation in which they announced a serious problem with the distribution of food in the East Bay, with central food committees being organized in each city's principal district.

On the morning of July 16 the general strike "officially" began with a walkout of the members of all unions that had voted in favor of the general strike, except for those needed to provide emergency services. About nineteen restaurants, services for the transport of milk, hospital services, and other essential activities continued to operate with the permission of the strike committee. The large department stores stayed open, but most of the smaller retail stores closed. The newspapers reported that some proprietors closed their businesses because strikers threatened them when they tried to stay open. In some small towns hundreds of miles away, agricultural production stopped because it could not be transported.[87]

The only reports of food rioting took place on the first day of the strike, the result of attempts by a store owner to profit as a result of the strike. Bridges proposed having union-controlled food depots throughout the city to prevent corrupt profiteering, and the *San Francisco Examiner* on July 16 announced that plans were being made to set up union-supervised food depots. The press also announced that a labor police force would patrol the city to contend with problems that might arise among strikers. Bars and night clubs were shut down, and the sale of liquor was prohibited by the strike committee. Writer Quinn described the atmosphere of the working-class communities: "Labor held the life-blood and energy. The owners remained in possession of the corpse. . . . Common social barriers [were] swept away in the spirit of the occasion. Strangers addressed each other warmly as old friends . . . [the workers'] minds were not inflamed with hysteria about bloody revolution, anarchy and chaos, as was the case with the businessmen and large numbers of white collar workers. To them the strikers were Joe, Bill, Mike, and Jerry, their pals, their neighbors, their benchmates. To them the hysterical pronouncement of the employers and civic officials, proclaiming that Moscow was trying to seize San Francisco as a colonial possession, were [*sic*] an amusing form of political delirium which had seized upon the upper classes."[88]

The degree of hysteria among some members of the business community should not be underestimated. Kenneth Kingsbury, the president of Standard Oil in California, in all seriousness tried to convince a representative of the Chamber of Commerce that the National Guard would not be able to stop the communists, whose long-planned "thing" would likely move from Seattle to Portland to Los Angeles.[89] Three thousand National Guard troops were stationed in San Francisco as Mayor Rossi declared a state of emergency.

On the first day of the general strike Governor Merriam made a radio address featuring narratives similar to those that had been used to discredit the Seattle general strike. He distinguished between "responsible" labor (those individuals who had been misled) and the radicals (those who were responsible for causing the problem). The public was assured that when the governor used repressive measures, he was acting to protect the citizenry's safety rather than on behalf of the employers, as unionists had claimed.

The employers and city officials continued to use the newspapers to bombard the public with antistrike editorials and articles. They also suggested the need for "citizens" to intervene to end the strike. During the week that the newspaper articles appeared, vigilantes attacked the offices of the Communist Party, the *Western Worker*, the Workers School, the MWIU, the ILA soup kitchen, and the Workers Ex-Servicemen's League. The attacks in San Francisco and other cities exhibited a pattern. The vigilantes would break in, attack the occupants, destroy property, and then leave. Immediately following each attack, the police would come and arrest the victims, who were then booked on vagrancy charges. The ILD provided bail for as many as it could until the bail fund was exhausted.[90]

Meanwhile the employers were doing everything they could to get the Roosevelt administration to intervene on their behalf. As the employers were told that Roosevelt was on board the U.S.S. *Houston* in the middle of the Pacific Ocean and thus couldn't be reached, they instead appealed to Secretary of Labor Frances Perkins, who refused to intervene. She insisted that this was a labor dispute, nothing more. In Washington there were mixed reactions on what to do. According to law, during general strikes the state and the federal government had the right to intervene. Apparently Secretary of State Cordell Hull, who was acting president while Roosevelt was on vacation, considered sending in the National Guard and the army to end the general strike. But Perkins insisted that the Roosevelt administration should not begin its tenure by "shooting it out with working people." She advised the president not to interrupt his vacation.[91]

The intention of the General Strike Committee's executive committee was to end the general strike. One of their first actions was to support a Public Utilities Commission resolution that the Municipal Railway Operators return to work immediately or be fired. Partial service was restored by the afternoon of the general strike's first day and full service by the second day, which made it appear as if the general strike was dissipating as soon as it began.[92]

The executive committee's next step was to loosen the restrictions on businesses by allowing more restaurants to open. The *San Francisco Chronicle* reported this action was intended to open all restaurants. By the evening of the second day the moderate executive committee urged arbitration against the vehement protests of Bridges and the workplace-democracy faction. The general strike had dissolved by its third day, July 19, because, according to the *Waterfront Worker*, labor officials were able to get control of it: "The General Strike was called off, not because a general strike cannot succeed, but because the fakers got control of the general strike committee."[93]

After the general strike the majority of longshoremen voted to accept arbitration, even though the seamen had yet to end their strike. The employers agreed to hire back all striking longshoremen. Word was received from Perkins that discrimination would not be permitted against the union members who had participated in the strike.[94] The seamen exhibited some hostility, despite Bridges's attempt to minimize the damage, but on July 31 they also returned to work.

POSTSTRIKE DEVELOPMENTS

The arbitration committee awarded a coastwide contract, wage increases, a reduction in work shift hours, and a hiring hall that was jointly controlled by the employers and the union but with an annually elected union dispatcher. Work assignments were allotted on a "rotary" basis, which ensured that all registered longshoremen had a chance to work before anyone was dispatched for a second time. In the past "troublemakers" (anyone who challenged working conditions) had been blacklisted. The rotary method with a union dispatcher prevented employer discrimination in hiring. The new hiring method allowed the former strike organizers to retain leadership positions within the union.

Shortly after the general strike press releases were sent out by the Merchants Committee and the California Convention of the American Legion. Their goals were to "strengthen immigration laws to prohibit persons of Communistic tendencies from entering the United States; to register, fingerprint and photograph all persons over eighteen; to amend the constitution to include seditious propaganda within the definition of treason; and to prohibit teaching communism in the schools."[95] The American Legion adopted three resolutions presented by the San Francisco Americanism Committee. The first was to censure Secretary of Labor Perkins for not deporting suspected communists during the strike; the second lauded the AFL leadership for its 100 percent Americanism; and the third requested that the state legislature enact a law punishing "radical agitation by death or one hundred years in jail."[96]

But these resolutions did not faze the new ILA union at the port of San Francisco. After the general strike militant direct action became informally institutionalized among the West Coast longshoremen, and "quickie strikes" were used to ensure the terms of the arbitration agreement. This change in power relations on the dock was quickly demonstrated to gang bosses who assumed that conditions would soon return to the "old days." In one poststrike incident a gang boss demanded an increase in the size of the sling loads or no one would work. When the longshoremen started to walk out, the irate gang boss "took a swing at the gang steward." In response the union representative grabbed him and wrestled him to the ground.[97] Things were never the same on the docks after the 1934 coastwide strike.

Bridges and the *Waterfront Worker* continued to promote racial inclusion in the ILA after the strike. Common to the discourses in the newsletter, racial solidarity was promoted through a rhetoric of class conflict and the equation of segregation with employer strategies. The newsletter said: "Obstacles standing out like mountains—this defines the racial prejudices, which have been so carefully guarded by the capitalist groups down through the ages. White trash will never agree to work with colored folks and the Negro must not attempt to introduce his presence into a group of white worker[s.] Just how carefully the employers have guarded these untrue statements has been unveiled in the recent Pacific

Coast strike. . . . There is just one fence—the minority group of capitalists on the one side; the workers including all casts and creeds on the other, with the power of a majority group."[98]

Despite periodic setbacks from other factions, continued progress toward racial inclusion was made at the San Francisco port after 1934. This was because of the rotary method of hiring with a union dispatcher, pressure from the workplace-democracy faction, and the continuing struggle for racial equality among African Americans within the union. The longshoremen's workplace-democracy faction also put pressure on the seamen's unions to be racially inclusive.[99]

The dual power rift between the workplace-democracy leadership of Local 38-79 and AFL officials caused considerable tension within the ILA and continued to do so for the next few years. After trying to change the AFL from within, the longshoremen eventually formed a new union— the International Longshoremen's and Warehousemen's Union (ILWU), which affiliated with the Congress of Industrial Organizations (CIO) in 1937. Participants in the rank-and-file strike committee during the general strike went on to become influential leaders in the new union. Harry Bridges became the president and was reelected for years.

Once the rank-and-file strike leaders accused of being communists gained power in the ILWU, they implemented practices very different from the ones communists had been accused of. Rather than centralizing power, they decentralized it and institutionalized practices that safeguarded democratic control of the union and through this the workplace by the rank and file. The terms of officers were reduced to one year, while "most locals established a limit of two consecutive terms for each office, after which incumbents either 'returned to the beach' as working longshoremen or sought some other elective positions . . . [and] salaries for all elected union officials were capped at no more than 10 percent of earnings of the highest paid workers."[100]

The fate of workplace-democracy political culture was very different after the San Francisco general strike in comparison with Seattle, where the metal trades strike was lost and labor resources declined. Because of the resources longshoremen gained through winning concessions, workplace-democracy principles and practices were institutionalized through the formation of the ILWU. Discursive strands and practices of the labor movement for the self-governing workshop continued to manifest themselves in this twentieth-century labor organization, although tensions among political factions continued. The new union selected the motto "An injury to one is an injury to all," expressing the inclusive industrial unionist narrative of the IWW, which had the same motto. The IWW's motto was in principle identical to the motto of the Knights before it: "An injury to one is the concern of all." Strikes continued on the waterfront in the following decades, but as Bridges observed: "Never again have the bosses dared to shoot our men down in cold blood."[101]

4 EXPLAINING GENERAL STRIKES

The Instrumentality of Culture

But I believe that the principles for which we fought in 1934 are still true and still useful. Whether your job is pushing a four wheeler or programming a computer, I don't know of any way for working people to win basic economic justice and dignity except by being organized into a solid, democratic union. . . . Sure, we may be taking a beating now, as we were in the years before 1934, but that's nothing new. What saved us then was our faith in each other, standing together despite what the employer did to intimidate and divide us, and to discredit our leadership. We showed the world that united working people could stand up against guns and tear gas, against the press and the courts, against whatever they threw at us. . . .

We can do it again. —*Harry Bridges, 1984*

Chapters two and three in this book have described the conditions that elicited general strikes in Seattle and San Francisco and how participants justified their actions. This chapter answers the third question posed at the outset: Was political culture, whether conservative or class-conscious, important at all? I answer this question through a multilevel comparative analysis of the configurations of economic, political, and historically contingent conditions in each case. Within this analysis I build a comparison of the political orientations of various labor factions and their differing responses to these conditions. Through this approach we can assess the instrumentality of workplace-democracy political culture in generating economic resources in the San Francisco case.

At the same time we can assess culture's symbiotic relationship with material resources in both the Seattle and San Francisco cases.

WORKPLACE-DEMOCRACY FACTIONS: EMERGENCE

Given the differing goals, strategies, and modes of organization of political factions within the same structural context, the impact of political culture can be gauged through asking if the general strikes in Seattle and San Francisco would have occurred without workplace-democracy factions. The answer is a cautious "no." Other labor factions either did not support having a general strike, or if they did, like the communists in San Francisco, they would likely not have been able to mobilize large numbers of workers because their rhetorical appeals (for example, those of the MWIU) were not resonant with most maritime workers. Communist Party (CP) organizers had to join with syndicalist-oriented rank-and-file longshoremen through the Albion Hall group to have an impact on the docks. To do this, they had to go against party directives of the centralized CP to work with West Coast longshoremen who valorized rank-and-file control.

Labor factions proposing resonant narratives, strategies, and modes of organization successfully mobilized the rank and file to challenge flagrant breaches of state neutrality in both the interception of Charles Piez's letter in Seattle and the shooting deaths of two protestors in San Francisco. At these historical moments workplace-democracy factions directed laborers' anger and did the organizational footwork to start a snowball effect of general strike momentum. At the Seattle Central Labor Council (SCLC) meeting it was the radical syndicalists within the metal trades unions and the Industrial Workers of the World (IWW) in the balconies who enthusiastically promoted a general strike referendum while the SCLC officials were away in Chicago. In San Francisco, when the coastwide longshoremen's strike began, the rank-and-file newsletter the *Waterfront Worker* had been proposing a general strike since as early as May 1934. Only when two workers were shot and killed and the National Guard was called in was the workplace-democracy faction able to mobilize unions to have general strike votes.

The events would not have inevitably led to general strikes if the moderate factions had been the majority in Seattle and San Francisco. These factions opposed having the general strikes because it violated the contracts of separate craft unions. The Holman faction in San Francisco rejected calling for a coastwide strike. Once Lee Holman was removed from his position, his ally Joseph Ryan (the moderate president of the national International Longshoremen's Association) opposed having a general strike. Given the dominance of a workplace-democracy political culture in Seattle, most moderates did vote to participate in a general strike once momentum began to snowball. However, it was the moderate International American Federation of Labor (AFL) officials who pressured many unions back to work in both Seattle and San Francisco.

If the officials on the SCLC had been present during the meeting in which the vote on a general strike referendum was taken in Seattle, they would likely have talked the rank and file out of it. Yet the ethos of rank-and-file control had such moral authority in Seattle that the SCLC officials respected the referendum process even though most thought a general strike at that time was a bad idea. Moreover, the SCLC officials did not try to undermine the general strike as did the moderate San Francisco Labor Council (SFLC).

The workplace-democracy factions were able to effectively mobilize labor in response to these events because there was a diffuse resonance for workplace-democracy narratives, strategies, and modes of organization among Seattle labor in 1919 and West Coast maritime workers in 1934. This resonance for rank-and-file control among Seattle labor allowed for the passage of a general strike referendum against the wishes of SCLC officials. It also provided the institutional opening for the workplace-democracy faction to gain leadership positions in the General Strike Committee, the Joint Marine Strike Committee (JMSC), and eventually the International Longshoremen's and Warehousemen's Union (ILWU).

It is beyond the scope of this research to say whether similar trajectories were present during the emergence of other American general strikes. What can be said is that had it not been for the workplace-democracy factions and a larger resonance for this political culture in both Seattle and San Francisco, it is extremely unlikely that these general strikes would have taken place. But the strategic impact of workplace-democracy political culture did not end with general strike emergence.

At first glance it appears that general strike outcomes can be explained by differences in economic structures and state actions—the more favorable economic bargaining position and state policies experienced by the longshoremen in San Francisco as opposed to the metal trades workers in post–World War I Seattle. This is, in fact, accurate. But a closer look reveals that political culture served as a foundation for gaining favorable state attention on the federal level and for creating economic bargaining chips that contributed to winning concessions as a result of the maritime and general strikes in San Francisco.

One obvious condition accounting for different outcomes was that the maritime workers in San Francisco had a more stable market position than the workers in Seattle, who were dependent on war production. Trade and the movement of cargo were essential to the commerce of San Francisco and other regions, including of course the other major port cities along the West Coast. For that reason the occupational need for maritime workers was secure despite the depression, although the working conditions were insecure, with unionists subject to wage decreases, workplace "speed-ups," and the "shape-up" method of hiring.

Because of the importance of maritime occupations to port commerce, the degree of impact was related to the successful maintenance of a coastwide strike organized on an industrial rather than a craft basis. Cargo could not simply be shipped to another port. The impact of the strike was maximized within the first few weeks when other trades joined the strike. The Teamsters refused to haul cargo on the waterfront, and the seamen and other maritime workers went out on strike for their own demands.

The creation of economic resources through the implementation of workplace-democracy strategies, organizational forms, and goals is directly related to the extent of concessions won. The federally appointed mediation committees did not simply hand over concessions like the first coastwide contract in American history to the International Longshoremen's Association (ILA). Only after a threatened coastwide strike did the first federal intervention take place, when President Roosevelt asked for a postponement and appointed a mediation committee. The concessions in the early agreements did not provide for a coastwide contract or joint control of the hiring hall with a union dispatcher, but the coastwide strike, riots, and general strike elicited increasingly generous concessions from the Roosevelt-appointed National Longshoremen's Board (NLB).

The success of the coastwide strike was achieved in part through the minimization of strike breaking by African-American workers. The degree of inclusion of African Americans and women varied in each case. The process of racial inclusion in the San Francisco case demonstrates the use of the workplace-democracy "cultural tool kit" to implement racial inclusion that contributed to strike success. Previous loss of strikes and organizing coastwide on an industrial basis served as a platform for appeals to racial inclusion and labor solidarity. Winning the concessions of joint control of the hiring hall with a union dispatcher and a rotary hiring system allowed for the retention of the workplace-democracy leadership after the strike, and for their continued pressure for racial inclusion. Although African Americans were marginalized, this changed over time because of their struggles within the union.

Favorable state actions were also indispensable to the success of this protracted coastwide strike. Once federal attention had been gained, the actions of President Roosevelt and Secretary of Labor Frances Perkins were crucial. As in Seattle the local and state politicians as well as the city, state, and national AFL officials who opposed the general strike tried to marginalize its leaders by characterizing them as "radicals" and "communists." But there was a difference in the response at the federal level. Perkins and Roosevelt did not accept these characterizations. Instead of sending in the army, they facilitated the success of the coastwide maritime strike and the general strike by refusing to intervene and appointing labor boards that granted increasingly generous concessions as events unfolded.

Ultimately, the coastwide strike would not have been successful without favorable state actions. But federal intervention would not have taken place had it not been for developments that were shaped by workplace-democracy strategies and practices, foremost rank-and-file control and the successful organization of an inclusive coastwide strike. The workplace-democracy faction and a resonance for this political culture were crucial to the success of the San Francisco general strike and the coastwide maritime strike.

While the success of the San Francisco case provides insights into the cultural foundation for the creation of resources, the failure of the Seattle general strike to win concessions and the outcomes in both cases shed light on the resource foundation of political cultures. First I address the need for a resource foundation to enable the communication of political culture and how the absence of such a foundation limited the strategic options of metal trades workers in Seattle. Then I analyze the relationship of resources to the communication, institutionalization, and demise of cultural forms in both Seattle and San Francisco.

The occurrence of a coastwide strike for common concessions was very different from a metal trades strike occurring within a single location. As previously mentioned, workplace-democracy political culture informed the organization, tactics, and goals of the unionists who organized the coastwide maritime strike. The response of maritime workers is, in part, explained by a resonance for this political culture. An awareness of this resonance helps us understand how political culture generated economic resources. But what is the relationship of resources to the presence and proliferation of political cultures?

The success, solidarity, and longevity of the coastwide strike were due to the degree of social and occupational networking, job interchangeability, and mobility among loggers from the Pacific Northwest with longshoremen and seamen at West Coast ports. The sense of collective identity and solidarity among West Coast unionists also grew out of a history of tension with East Coast AFL officials. Seattle labor prioritized local control and autonomy, which facilitated a stronger identification with local and regional union organizations than with the Internationals.

Although workplace-democracy tendencies were apparent in Seattle and among longshoremen before the 1920s, a richer network for cultural diffusion had emerged by that time. There were two reasons for this: first, Seattle had become a stronghold for the IWW during the second decade of the twentieth century; and second, the IWW's Marine Transport Workers Industrial Union was founded, with its recruitment of hundreds of West Coast longshoremen between 1919 and 1921. Furthermore, historical lessons had been learned in the wake of the Seattle general strike and the 1919 ILA strike. Through occupational networks the communication of workplace-democracy narratives and lessons of past strikes paved the way for the organization of the coastwide maritime strike and the San Francisco general strike.

It is important to emphasize that the characteristics that facilitated coastwide organization and solidarity, in which workplace-democracy culture was instrumental, were endemic to West Coast maritime unionism. Although this is not the only region in which workplace-democracy cultures flourished, the clustering and proliferation of this cultural form in this region was made possible through occupational interchange and networking specific to the West Coast geography. The resources and organizational context that these jobs provided served as the foundation for the material diffusion of political culture. This type of occupational interchange did not exist among East Coast occupations. Longshoremen and seamen led separate lives, and there was no logging industry similar to that in Seattle, where radical industrial unionists had established unions.[1]

The *Seattle Union Record* did mention an attempt to organize a shutdown of shipyards in the Pacific Northwest, but this never materialized. Ultimately, West Coast metal trades workers, as opposed to those in the maritime occupations, could not draw on a common political culture and shared orientation toward strategies because they were not in occupations that were interchangeable or that directly linked them in some way. The cultural communication that allowed for strategic success and solidarity among widely dispersed maritime workers was dependent on specific resources for the communication of culture that did not exist among the West Coast metal trades workers.

Furthermore, the various maritime unions sought to gain concessions from the success of a coastwide strike because of the experience of common grievances. But it was exclusively the Puget Sound shipyard workers who had a wage decrease implemented by the federal government. Shipyard workers at other ports had nothing to gain from a coastwide strike except a show of solidarity. It is difficult enough to organize strikes and maintain solidarity when participants have something concrete to gain. But given both the lack of concessions to be gained for unionists at other ports and the absence of workplace networks in the metal trades industry, the occurrence of a coastwide strike of all shipyard workers in 1919 was not feasible.

Finally, state actors making decisions within the political climate of the New Deal were indispensable to success in the San Francisco case, whereas Seattle metal trades workers faced a repressive state and postwar political climate. In addition to the inevitable decrease in production because of the end of World War I, Seattle suffered from being targeted by the federal government. Ship contracts were canceled as a punishment for the general strike, and a poststrike depression followed that was more severe in Seattle than at other ports. The forces of state repression and the political climate largely determined the outcome in the Seattle case.

INSTITUTIONALIZATION AND DEMISE

In the Seattle and San Francisco cases there was a tight link among resources, occupational networks, and the flourishing or demise of political cultures. Workplace-democracy tendencies were apparent among Seattle unionists before the war years. But from 1914 to 1919, Seattle's radical political culture flourished because of the resources from state-subsidized jobs for war production and the attraction of radicals to industries in which workers were not subject to conscription. The already left-leaning labor culture in Seattle flourished with the growth of numerous new worker enterprises, organizations, and mass meetings.

As mentioned earlier, Seattle experienced the postwar depression and closing of its government-subsidized industries sooner than other West Coast ports. Most radical workers, who had been drawn to the nonconscription status of war production industries, left Seattle to find jobs elsewhere. Many workers' enterprises that formed during the war production years, and some that formed shortly after the general strike, went under because of a loss of resources and activists dedicated to their success. Repressive state actions and economic decline contributed to the loss of occupational resources and to the demise of workplace-democracy culture among Seattle labor.

In San Francisco, however, the relationship of political and economic resources to the fate of workplace-democracy culture was very different. Although the maritime workers had exhibited workplace-democracy characteristics early in their history, it wasn't until 1933 and 1934 that these tendencies were harnessed into a powerful and successful coastwide movement. This occurred, in part, because of the political resources provided by Section 7a of the National Industrial Recovery Act (NIRA), passed in the summer of 1933. A workplace-democracy political culture flourished through the distribution of the *Waterfront Worker*, the dynamics of the rank-

and-file convention, as well as the polarization and solidarity produced through the coastwide maritime strike, the riots, and the general strike.

Once the longshoremen agreed to accept arbitration and go back to work, the NLB ruled that there would be joint control of the hiring hall by both longshoremen and employers but with a union dispatcher. As a result of the new method of hiring, the employers could no longer black-list troublemakers by excluding them during the shape-up. The fact that the workplace-democracy faction was able to maintain leadership positions within the ILA after the general strike was crucial to the institutionalization of some workplace-democracy narratives and practices in the subsequent formation of the ILWU.

After the general strike workplace-democracy principles were both informally and formally institutionalized among longshoremen. Militant direct action among the rank and file was informally institutionalized as longshoremen, previously resigned to abusive conditions, orchestrated spontaneous walkouts if demands were not met. The ILWU organized as an industrial union, codifying into its constitution the principles of rank-and-file control, union autonomy within federations, and the One Big Union tradition that was inclusive of race and nationality as well as a rhetoric of class conflict. The connection between the citizen/workers and civic commitment, so important to the nineteenth-century movement for a self-governing workshop, is apparent in the preamble of the ILWU's constitution: "Since the beginning of history, mankind has struggled individually and collectively for political, economic and cultural betterment, and has found the greatest ability to make such advancement through democratic organization to achieve common aims. Therefore, we who have the common objectives to advance the living standards of ourselves and our fellow workers everywhere in the world, to promote the general welfare of our nation and our communities, to banish racial and religious prejudice and discrimination, to strengthen democracy everywhere and to achieve permanent peace in the world, do form ourselves into one, indivisible union and adopt the following constitution to guide our conduct and protect our democracy within the union."[2]

These and other principles were reaffirmed by the ILWU at the Tenth Biennial Convention, held in San Francisco in 1953:

[Rank & File Control/Organizational Autonomy]
    A union is built on its members. The strength, understanding and unity

of the membership can determine the union's course and its advancements. . . . In brief, it is the membership of the union which is the best judge of its own welfare; not the officers, not the employers, not politicians. . . . Above all this approach is based on the conviction that given the truth and an opportunity to determine their own course of action, the rank and file in 99 cases out of a hundred will take the right path in their own interests and in the interests of other people.

[One Big Union]

Labor unity is at all times the key for a successful economic advancement—anything that detracts from labor unity hurts all labor . . .

Workers are indivisible. There can be no discrimination because of race, color, creed, national origin, religious or political belief. Any division among workers can help no one but the employers . . .

To help any worker in distress must be a daily guide in the life of every trade union and its individual members. Labor solidarity means just that. Unions have to accept the fact that the solidarity of labor stands above all else, including even the so-called sanctity of contract. . . . Every picket line must be respected as if it were our own . . .

[Rhetoric of Class Conflict]

The days are gone when a union can consider dealing with single employers. The powerful financial interests of the country are bound together in every conceivable type of united organization to promote their own welfare and to resist the demands of labor. . . . The employers of this country are part of a well organized, carefully coordinated, effective fighting machine. They can be met only on equal terms, which requires industry-wide bargaining and the most extensive economic strength of organized labor.[3]

It is outside the scope of this book to comment on the viability of workplace-democracy culture among West Coast longshoremen beyond the 1930s. It is worth noting, however, that in the "epochal" Mechanization and Modernization Agreement that the ILWU and the Pacific Maritime Association signed in 1960, the employers had to pay the unionists for replacing their jobs with technology. This was accomplished through a fund to which employers were required to contribute at a rate of five million dollars a year. It was not a profit-sharing plan. Rather, the contributions came from money saved through the implementation of labor-saving devices, which the employers were entitled to innovate under the agreement. The purpose of the plan was to supplement earnings on the job if it became necessary.

In the ILWU newsletter *The Dispatcher* ILWU librarian Gene Vrana described the principle underlying the agreement as the "revolutionary concept that a registered longshoreman owned his job for life or would be well compensated if he lost it through mechanization."[4] This concept bears a resemblance to those of artisan producers during the Jacksonian era who claimed that a worker's labor was his or her own "property."

CONCLUSION

The ways that regional political cultures inform labor strategies and goals over generations merit closer examination. This two-tiered comparative analysis has illustrated that the geographical presence of certain types of political cultures can make a difference in the success or failure of collective action. Political culture, however, was animated through the agency of labor factions that were socially located in relation to resources, social and geographical networks, and institutional power. Regional traditions of rank-and-file control in Seattle and West Coast maritime unions allowed the workplace-democracy factions to gain positions of power to mobilize workers through resonant workplace-democracy narratives and practices. The trajectories of action that resulted from the workplace-democracy worldview were different from what would have resulted had other factions gained control whose cultural understanding of the world and laborers' place in it were different.

5 THE MAKING OF MORAL CERTITUDE

Institutions, Identities, and Resonance

> Lay down true principles and adhere to them inflexibly. Do not
> be frightened into their surrender by the alarms of the timid, or
> the croakings of wealth against the ascendancy of the people.
>
> —*Thomas Jefferson, 1816*

In this book we have looked at the instrumentality of political culture in the construction of resonant discourses and practices that mobilized the rank and file during the Seattle and San Francisco general strikes. Economic resources were generated through political culture in the San Francisco case. In this final chapter I suggest several ways to think about the links among cultural resonance, institutions, and the identities of American workers that are relevant to mobilization for workplace empowerment in the twenty-first century.

CULTURE MATTERS

The instrumental role of culture in Seattle in 1919 and San Francisco in 1934 supports the argument for a preexisting cultural resonance, which informed the narratives, strategies, and modes of organization of workplace-democracy factions and the mobilization of the rank and file. Without question, strategies were formulated in response to economic, political, and organizational opportunities and constraints, but these formulations were mediated through the cultural lenses of political orientations, some of which were more resonant than others within Pacific Northwest and West Coast occupations.

Although the impact of culture and identity has been taken more seriously in the past few decades, much of the existing labor literature continues to privilege structural determinism. Research that claims an autonomous impact for political culture differs from recent studies that explain labor protest as emerging through a kind of "spontaneous generation" through the process of collective action or research that sees strategies as emerging from organizational logic, with cultural "impulses" playing a secondary role. Sociologist Rick Fantasia's *Cultures of Solidarity: Consciousness, Action, and Contemporary American Workers* provides an example of the argument for spontaneous generation.[1] He is critical of both a static survey approach to class consciousness and the Leninist emphasis on the need for an external vanguard party to produce consciousness that moves past bread-and-butter issues.[2] Rather, within the process of collective struggle "militant action creates a context in which ideas may emerge, change and be subjected to scrutiny and renegotiation."[3]

Fantasia's study analyzes what he has called "cultures of solidarity." By this he means "a cultural expression that arises within the wider culture, yet is emergent in its embodiment of oppositional practices and meanings." These new practices include "tactical activities, organizational forms, and institutional arrangements" that create solidarity through mobilization and engagement with opponents. The production of these cultures is contingent on preexisting institutional arrangements and emergent values of solidarity and moral outrage. Fantasia accurately recognizes that changes in beliefs occur through polarized collective action, but the content of the preexisting culture of activists, its notions of justice, do not appear to make much difference in the kinds of oppositional meanings the collective action generates.[4]

The latter approach, which argues that the organizational logic at the point of production most determines strategy, is apparent in historical sociologist Howard Kimeldorf's book *Battling for American Labor: Wobblies, Craft Workers, and the Making of the Union Movement.*[5] Challenging proponents of American exceptionalism who conclude that American labor is conservative, his analysis explains why dockworkers in Philadelphia and hotel and restaurant workers in New York left the Industrial Workers of the World (IWW) to join the American Federation of Labor (AFL) early in the twentieth century. Kimeldorf insightfully recognizes a "syndicalist impulse" among both the IWW's revolutionary industrial unions and the moderate business unions of the AFL. He argues that proponents of American exceptionalism have missed these syndicalist inclinations because of their search for a "classless" national value system. However, in his efforts to debunk the psychological reductionism of the American exceptionalism school, Kimeldorf concludes that the "syndicalist impulse" can better be explained through organizational logic than national culture. Despite the numerous insights both these excellent studies provide, they downplay the origins, internal logic, and autonomous impact of cultural forms—the ways that preexisting cultural texts are linked to identity and facilitate or constrain the content of insurrectionary narratives and practices.

It is true that direct action and the organizational logic of industrial unionism made more sense to less skilled and disenfranchised workers: immigrants, women, people of color, and some Euro-American males. Yet granting that labor factions recognize an organizational logic to the production process does not mean that goals, strategies, and modes of organization were not culturally mediated. This study of general strikes indicates otherwise. We can conclude three things from it. First, within the same unions (organizational structures) the political orientations (cultural understandings) of different factions mediated their selection of goals, strategies, and modes of organization. Second, there was a relationship between the availability of workplace-democracy "cultural material" within geographical regions and occupations and the adoption and reconfiguration of these resonant narrative and strategic repertoires. Third, the resonance of workplace-democracy narratives fostered a "moral certitude" among labor organizers and much of the rank and file that justified their challenges to workplace disempowerment.

One thing we can conclude from this book is that narratives with the moral authority to justify engaging in general strikes refracted the national traditions from which they were derived. Could we be throwing out the "cultural" baby with the "conservative" American exceptionalism bath water? In this final chapter I propose three speculative arguments for consideration in light of this study, which also move beyond it. The goal is to prompt a rethinking of the premises of American exceptionalism, its unquestioning acceptance, as well as its adamant rejection.

First I argue that effective mobilization for these general strikes required more than emergent oppositional meanings or strategies derived from the organizational logic of the production process. It required an alternative worldview through which moral certitude was derived from beliefs and values that informed the workers' identities. Second, American labor did exhibit antistate orientations distinct from those of "class-conscious Europeans." Historically Americans accepted municipal and federal ownership of some "public" industries, but not state ownership of the means of production or workplaces. This antistatist proclivity was related to the role of land in the political economy of the United States (discussed in chapter one), the organization of the state, and a legal system that privileged private property as the foundation of citizenship. Third, among other twentieth-century developments the changing meaning of socialism since the post-Lenin era has contributed to the distancing of American labor from the left, with some exceptions during the Great Depression. I conclude by suggesting that progressives rethink routes to economic and political equality through drawing on narratives from the early republic, foremost those of Jefferson and Paine, and the labor movement for the self-governing workshop in innovative ways.

THE MORAL AUTHORITY OF WORKPLACE DEMOCRACY

Scholars have analyzed the ways that movements construct mobilization appeals from traditional cultural texts, "mentalities," and life experiences.[6] Mobilization appeals are assessed according to the degree to which they are resonant with individual and collective identities. Yet identities are much more than the ways that individuals or groups negotiate self- and public definitions of common grievances and interests. Identity constitutes a nexus for the fulfillment of human needs through individual and collective worldviews constructed through available cultural material. These human needs take the form of biological requirements (food, shelter), epistemological security (a coherent worldview that sustains identities), and status (or self- and social valuation). Individuals and collectivities appropriate and reconstruct the cultural material available given their social and geographical locations to provide "emotional management" in the ongoing struggle to fulfill human needs, given life conditions within varying social locations. Appropriated narratives and practices offer solace for economic and status deprivations or provide justifications for good fortune and access to abundant resources. Not doing this "cultural work" has such emotional consequences as anxiety, despair, depression, even suicide.

The interrelationship of these needs and how they are emotionally managed through identities and worldviews merits serious attention by social movement analysts. A more in-depth explication is beyond the scope of this book. It is sufficient to recognize that human beings do not sacrifice and die for economic interests alone. They challenge, sacrifice, and die for what they believe is the truth, which derives from moral authority deeply rooted within one's understandings of justice and injustice. It is this moral authority that puts "iron in the souls" of those who challenge the social order. This moral certainty was exhibited by workplace-democracy factions within both general strikes.[7] But where do the understandings of justice come from? Looking at the social construction and internalization of "moral codes" provides a first step for answering this question.

All societies construct cultural systems to mediate goal-directed activities that sustain social life. No human being who engages in social interaction (with the possible exception of a feral child) has failed to internalize a cultural map of how the world works and his or her place in it. Cultural explanations are constructed to legitimate social rules, especially the distribution of resources, status, and power within stratified societies. All societies construct rights and obligations among their members, and through this process notions of justice and injustice emerge. The rules constructed to coordinate social institutions and interaction result in "moral codes."[8] I am not prepared to say exactly how deeply embedded these moral codes are. Do they organize human social psychology as we biologically interact with the environment, through which we become internally "wired"? Are they unconscious frames like the rhetorical ones that funnel how we see the world?[9] We do know that moral codes are embedded within cultural institutions, narratives, and practices and are drawn on by individuals and collectivities to construct identities.

Human beings form a sense of identity through social interaction and communication, foremost by way of verbal and written language.[10] Through the process of developing an identity, the rules of society, its expectations, and obligations are learned. As people within highly stratified societies grow, the self becomes constituted through a nexus of identities internalized through institutions and other organized activities as well as the cultural narratives and practices that constitute them.[11] Embedded within these organized activities are family narratives, workplace narratives, national narratives, and other narratives learned in educational institutions and community groups as well as through mass media. All narratives contain heroines and heroes and villains. They tell us about our society's and community's history and leaders, what is right and wrong, and what we should value and dislike.

The identities of workers may therefore be constituted through dominant national and civic as well as racialized and gendered narratives and practices, which affect workplace interaction, labor mobilization, and solidarity. Laborers cannot be extracted out of the extra-institutional contexts through which their identities have been formed. *Through these identities there is a resonance for some cultural narratives and practices, as opposed to others, ones that are familiar and evoke emotional attachments to symbols, groups, and ways of life.* Consequently, there is such a thing as a national political culture with a "thin coherence."[12]

Does a resonance for national and civic narratives mean that American workers were (or are) inclined to conservative political orientations, as the American exceptionalism school has argued? *The answer lies in the refraction of these national and civic narratives, which are resonant with American class identities.* The potential for conservative refraction obviously exists and is currently drawn on by neoliberals. But national narratives have also refracted liberal to radically egalitarian models of democracy, as the movement for the self-governing workshop and these two case studies have demonstrated. How national narratives are refracted depends in part on the access to resources, technology, and cultural material available to working people given their social and regional locations. As mentioned in chapter one, the progressive labor organizations with the largest mass followings in U.S. history were the Knights of Labor and the Populist Party. Activists mobilized people concerned about dispossession of land, skills, and livelihood through capitalist industrialization and an increasingly powerful merchant capitalist class. But could this mobilization also have been related to the narratives and practices of workplace-democracy culture, which provided a moral certitude through its resonance with dominant national narratives while at the same time providing an alternative worldview in which labor empowerment was central?

The workplace-democracy lineage is notable for its "moral inventiveness . . . [the activists' ability] to fashion from existing cultural traditions historically new standards of condemnation of what exists."[13] Most workplace-democracy activists in Seattle and San Francisco did not adhere to rigid ideological doctrines or belong to political parties. Nor were they moderates who resigned themselves to "the way it is." These labor cultures were animated through activists who drew on eclectic theoretical sources to make sense of their life conditions. There were lively debates at meetings and in labor media about political philosophy and international events. These were "full spectrum" political cultures that included a viable political left whose proposals other factions at times supported and at other times rejected. The left factions infused the labor cultures with imagination, innovation, and radical producerist narratives that morally justified the right of laborers to control the workplace. The practice of rank-and-file decision making was essential to the vibrancy of political cultures in Seattle and San Francisco. The policies workers argued about and votes they cast made a real difference in the governance of their unions.

But if the narratives and practices that constituted workplace democracy cultures provided moral certitude, this was due to its resonance with identities formed through the organization of life within the political and economic institutions of American society. The "Americanism" of workplace-democracy cultures, the resonance for participatory democracy, local control, and receiving the fruits of labor explain why it caught on and made such an impact, as opposed to ideologies that sounded alien and unrealistic.

STATE ORGANIZATION

The class structure and revolutionary struggle through which the Constitution was produced had implications for the resonance of American class identities with the pursuit of private property and wariness of centralized state power. Labor analyst Mike Davis has pointed out that with the exception of the American Revolution, bourgeois revolutions have depended heavily for their success on the lower classes. Artisans did participate in the revolution, as noted in chapter one, but colonial revolutionaries were disproportionately from the American bourgeois, large merchants, capitalist landowners, and planters. Furthermore, the revolutionary bourgeoisie in the United States was able to "consolidate hegemony" with "exceptional class alliances." The numerical dominance of small capitalist farmers had no equivalent in mid-nineteenth-century Europe (where agriculture was predominantly conducted by semiaristocratic landowners or peasants). This provided support for politics that celebrated the unchallenged sanctity of private property.[14]

In his *Law and the Shaping of the American Labor Movement*, scholar William E. Forbath stated that the framers of the Constitution (Jefferson and Paine were not among them) rejected the centralized organization of government that had been evolving in Europe in the late eighteenth century. "As Madison's *Federalist No. 10* illustrates," writes Forbath, "some of the framers were haunted by the specter of enduring political 'factions' based on economic condition—above all factions based on the propertyless. A poor or propertyless faction could constitute a voting majority and seek to use the state to despoil the propertied or shirk its own economic obligations. Already the framers had seen this happen in the new republics. Partly to avert such politics, they created a constitutional scheme that treated the sphere of common law rights of contract and property as a suprapolitical realm to private right. As far as market and property and, therefore, class relations were concerned, the rules of the game were presumptively matters of law and not politics, matters of courts, not legislatures."[15]

The "canonization" of private property in the Constitution to benefit the elite gentry and the "democratizing" role of land (dating back to the early republic envisioned by Jefferson and Paine) resulted in a discursive dovetailing of support for property rights that refracted different understandings. Land was the route to independence and equality in an agrarian country of small worker-owners. Family narratives, illustrated through strike participant Hulet Wells's experience (quoted extensively in chapter two), idealized agrarian landownership as freedom compared with wage slavery and unemployment. The defense of "property" within national, regional, and family narratives meant something different to those who were concentrating their wealth and power through new hereditary "aristocracies."

The legal privileging of property rights sounded the death knell for the labor movement and for the self-governing workshop with the emergence of large corporations and monopolies after the Civil War. At that time the legal system gave corporations rights as "individuals," creating another legal obstacle to workplace democracy. The degree to which the state intervened in labor disputes to the disadvantage of workers can be missed when focusing exclusively on legislative and executive actions, but "if one includes judicial actions and the role of legal discourse and judge-made state policy, the picture changes dramatically."[16]

The framers' distrust of centralized power, be it a mercantilist state or a wealthy elite, is evident in the narratives and practices of artisan republicanism and the labor movement for the self-governing workshop. It is important to recognize that this apprehension took many forms and did *not* preclude a positive role for government in promoting the public good and regulating monopolies so long as the government or the municipal, state, or federal levels remained within popular control.[17] The Knights of Labor supported state ownership of a few "public" industries, such as utilities and transportation. The National Labor Union (NLU) rejected state ownership of growing monopolies in the 1860s,[18] although it was during the nineteenth and early twentieth centuries that socialism had the largest following among Americans.

THE CHANGING MEANING OF SOCIALISM

One of the differences that historical sociologist Kim Voss has recognized between American workers and those of France and England in the nineteenth century was stronger antistatist sentiments among Americans.[19] However, she argues that Americans did exhibit a class consciousness not so different from workers in European countries. As mentioned in chapter two, Socialist candidate Eugene Debs received 6 percent of the popular vote in 1912, and socialists have won seats in numerous municipal elections in the United States. It was really after World War I that these tendencies declined, however, with some exceptions during the Great Depression. Does this mean that at one time U.S. workers were more open to state-centered socialist alternatives?

Certainly some members of the working class have supported state ownership and control of the means of production and centralized reorganization of the economy, to create a socialist state. But it is imperative to recognize that today's popular conception of "socialism" is different from what it meant before and shortly after World War I and the Russian revolution. At that time socialism was commonly understood as workers' direct control and management of the industries in which they worked. "Public" ownership sometimes referred to the municipality or state rather than the federal government.

When state ownership was proposed for the public interest, the goal was to prohibit the private appropriation of local resources by absentee owners or monopolists who charged exorbitant prices. For example, in 1919 the magazine *The Survey* described a plan advanced for public control of the railroads by its employees as the "most daring proposition of its kind ever . . . [offered] as a practical measure." *The Survey* went on to say that the proposal differed from Bolshevism because it included the "higher officials of the railroads in the plan for the direction and control of the transportation business of the country by the people actually engaged in it."[20]

This change in the popular understanding of socialism in the United States since the post-Lenin era has not received the attention it deserves, although some scholars have recognized similar changes in other countries. Describing France, historian William Sewell Jr. has noted that the vision of a "republic of labor . . . founded on democratic and republican corporations, organized as producers associations and linked through elected representatives into a solidarity worker's state," remained firmly rooted among numerous labor and socialist movements until the outbreak of World War I. As a result of the Bolshevik revolution and the founding of the Communist Party, "French Socialism definitely abandoned the corporate socialist vision it had assumed after 1848."[21] In nineteenth-century England socialists Sidney and Beatrice Webb proposed establishing a "Grand National Consolidated Trades Union" in which "the instruments of production were to become the property, not of the whole community, but of the particular set of workers who used them."[22]

What is unusual is that this vision lasted longer in the United States than in other industrial nations. Labor scholar Bruce Laurie has argued that the durability of this type of producerist radicalism "inhibited the transition to socialism." Whereas radical republicanism developed into republican socialism in France after 1850, the furthest that producerist radicalism got was making proposals to nationalize some public industries because it never accepted the state as an "instrument for class liberation." The reason there was no socialism in America, according to Laurie, is that "radicalism" or the movement for the self-governing workshop was so strong.[23]

Workers throughout the world applauded the Bolshevik revolution in 1917. Seattle labor celebrated it as the first "workers state," and the *Seattle Union Record* updated workers about developments there. But Seattle supporters did not associate the Russian revolution with the state-centralized, bureaucratic regime it was to become. The IWW newsletter *The Industrial Worker* stated in 1919 that "Bolshevik Soviets are politico-industrial groupings of representatives of the producers in Russia," a description not so different from the anarcho-syndicalism they promoted.[24]

This early perception of the Russian revolution was also prevalent among the British and Italian workers. Scholar Miriam Golden has pointed out that between 1917 and the early 1920s, the revolution was understood by workers movements in these countries "as the culmination of the Soviet struggle for power, aimed at the direct control of industry by the workers." This differs from today's perception of Leninism as "primarily a justification for the strict subordination of affiliated organizations, including trade unions, to a revolutionary party."[25] There are many possible reasons for the late-twentieth-century decline in support for socialism by American laborers. Could one of them be related to an aversion to centralized control, given national and civic narratives and historical experiences?

RETHINKING ROUTES TO ECONOMIC AND POLITICAL EQUALITY

Let's presume it is accurate that political culture has an autonomous effect in social movement mobilization and in the selection of strategies and that twentieth-century American workers have a resonance for workplace-democracy cultures because of identities formed through national narratives and socializing institutions in the United States. Then shouldn't American movements, concerned with increasing economic and political equality, rethink how debates have been framed and consider alternative proposals to achieve social change? Shouldn't we reconsider the narratives of the early republic, especially those of Jefferson and Paine, and the nineteenth-century labor movement for the self-governing workshop, given their resonance with American class identities? A number of arguments could be made against doing this. Below I respond to two of these.

First, some people have an understandable reaction of dismissal to the narratives of "the framers" and nineteenth-century Euro-American labor organizations because of their exploitation of African slaves, indigenous populations, and women in the name of reason, progress, democracy, and land rights. The American Enlightenment thought of Jefferson, himself a slave owner, and Paine, as well as Enlightenment thought in general, has been dismissed because of its use to justify the domination and exploitation of others. Yet beliefs that domination and exploitation are wrong, and that all people should be free to determine the course of their lives, derive from Western democratic Enlightenment values, specifically a concern for autonomy and equality. The contradictions of the Enlightenment tradition remain within American class identities formed through institutions that perpetuate discriminatory narratives and practices, but these contradictions have also generated egalitarian movements that challenge them. Only movements that name and openly struggle with the contradictions of the Enlightenment legacy will be able to successfully mobilize broad national and global coalitions to create social change.[26]

Culture, language, and both conscious and unconscious practices communicate and reinforce gendered and racialized power relations in the workplace and other informal settings. Organizing based on economic reductionist goals, which dismiss the importance of culture and thereby mask the dominance of Euro-American males, will fail to create the solidarity, participatory democracy, and zeitgeist needed to create fundamental change in a global world. Invoking Jefferson and Paine and the movement for the self-governing workshop allows us to present challenges to the culture of contradiction as part of the American heritage, not as ideas in opposition to it.

And now, the second argument: As mentioned in chapter one, the nineteenth-century labor movement for the self-governing workshop has been dismissed as both "backward looking" (because it was promoted when society was not fully industrialized) and bourgeois (through its acceptance of capitalist market relations). Yet the political principles that informed Jefferson's and Paine's egalitarian visions of a republic are no more archaic than are the political principles that informed the Declaration of Independence, which was written in the same time period. Why is a society that morally values commitment to the public good, has minimal income and wealth divisions, in which *all* citizens have state-secured access to land or money as their birthright, any less "realistic" than socialism? The model may be "bourgeois" through a European class-consciousness lens, but it fundamentally challenged monopoly capitalism through the demand for an equitable distribution of resources and power for labor and the protection of the public sphere. In fact, the governing principles and economic organization proposed by Jefferson and Paine are at odds with current neoliberal policies that foster the concentration of wealth and power in the name of "liberty" and "property."

I cannot emphasize enough that if movements do succeed at mobilizing broad coalitions through a resonance for workplace-democracy narratives, such mobilization is not a guarantee of successful outcomes. Workplace-democracy organizations and activists learned the lessons of state and employer repression throughout American history. Without resources and without careful strategic analysis of political, economic, and cultural opponents at every stage, a movement, notwithstanding its moral certitude, is sure to fail.

These two West Coast general strikes provide lessons about the mobilization potential of a political culture that refracts, from the life experience of laborers, deeply resonant traditions. During the Seattle general strike the enthusiasm generated by workplace-democracy visions of social transformation and a worldwide zeitgeist of insurrection triumphed over caution about labor's postwar economic and political vulnerability. Economic forces and state actors combined to undermine the resources that fueled a vital workplace-democracy culture. But the San Francisco general strike had a different outcome. The pragmatic radicalism of workplace-democracy strategists produced a successful outcome. The result was the dignity of greater worker control over the labor process, a higher standard of living, and a union culture supporting civic commitment, inclusion, and workplace democracy.

I am not arguing that worker co-ops—or worse yet, hierarchically organized employee-owned businesses—are solutions to the problems of labor exploitation. I am arguing that the political theories of Jefferson, Paine, and the movement for the self-governing workshop are rich with resonant narratives and practices that could be framed in innovative ways to address labor disempowerment and other inequalities in the twenty-first century. Awakening the sleeping memory of workplace democracy and radical producerism, with its moral economy of just and unjust accumulation, could provide a vision of change with the moral authority to challenge neoliberal narratives that legitimate the concentration of wealth and power among global corporate oligarchies.

There is much more heritage to reclaim and historical memory to restore. As the culture of contradictions continues to generate the ongoing process of democratization, the question is not whether we can create the "ideal" agrarian society of Jefferson and Paine. Rather, the question is whether the authority of their vision can provide the moral certitude for all citizens to claim the equitable distribution of power and propertied independence that is their heritage.

NOTES

1 NEW WINE IN OLD BOTTLES

The chapter epigraphs are from the following sources: Thomas Jefferson, Letter to Thomas Cooper, 1814, "Thomas Jefferson on Politics & Government," available online at etext.virginia.edu/jefferson/quotations/jeffcont.htm; accessed in May 2005. Thomas Paine, *Agrarian Justice* (1796), reprinted in Foner, *Life and Major Writings of Thomas Paine.*

1. See Lakoff, *Don't Think of an Elephant,* as well as his *Moral Politics;* Block, *Vampire State;* and T. Frank, *What's the Matter with Kansas?*

2. Werner Sombart's 1906 book *Why Is There No Socialism in the United States?* (reprinted in 1976) is commonly cited as the origin of the American exceptionalism debate.

3. Various explanations have been proposed for the different political orientations of American workers. They include the lack of pronounced class stratification (thus there is no history of feudalism) to generate a collective identity as a subordinate class; the privileging of individualism and private property within the Constitution and the Bill of Rights; early suffrage of male workers (whereas the struggle for suffrage had been a source of working-class solidarity in many European societies); greater access to land and overall prosperity in the United States in comparison with Europe; the escape valve of the West (which provided alternatives to challenging exploitative conditions); generational waves of immigration, creating racial and ethnic rivalries; the existence of slavery during working-class formation, resulting in racism that undermined class solidarity; and twentieth-century changes in workplace organization. For discussions of these explanations, see Lipset, *American Exceptionalism;* Roediger, *Wages of Whiteness;*

Davis, *Prisoners of the American Dream;* Laslett and Lipset, *Failure of a Dream;* and Gordon et al., *Segmented Work, Divided Workers.*

4. A student of labor historian John Common[s], [Selig] Perlman contributed to the Commons Institutional school. See Perlman, *Theory of the Labor Movement,* and Common[s]'s four volumes of *History of the Labor Movement in the United States.*

5. Perlman, *Theory of the Labor Movement,* 190.

6. Ibid., 159–60.

7. What may have been the first general strike in America occurred in Philadelphia in 1835 during a spontaneous walk-out of roughly a dozen trades in support of the ten-hour day. Apparently business was "brought to a stand-still." Given the ambiguity about whether this actually was a general strike, this walk-out was left out of the count, although it is mentioned in Crook, *Communism and the General Strike,* and Foner, *History of the Labor Movement in the United States,* vol. 5, *The AFL in the Progressive Era, 1910–1915.*

8. This count of twenty-one is derived from Bing, *War-Time Strikes and Their Adjustments;* Crook, *Communism and the General Strike;* Fantasia, *Cultures of Solidarity;* Lannon, "Oakland and the General Strike of 1946 Remembered"; Lipsitz, *Rainbow at Midnight;* and Larry, "Class Conflict." Larry's count of general strikes differs from mine due to different definitions of this tactic. The strikes in Springfield, Illinois; Kansas City, Kansas; Billings, Montana; and Waco, Texas, are cited in Bing, *War-Time Strikes and Their Adjustments,* 30, note 1. This is the only account of these strikes in the existing literature. Based on Bing's characterization of them as general strikes, I include these here with the caution that one or more may have simply been industrywide strikes rather than general strikes, according to the definition I have used in this book.

9. Americans have frequently participated in militant strikes, which have been both protracted and violent. But militancy, which means being combative or aggressive to further a cause, should not be confused with radicalism, which seeks to transform the organization of society. The lack of a demand for structural transformation in the relations between capital and labor has been a distinguishing characteristic of American unions in the twentieth century.

10. See Montgomery, *Worker's Control in America.* Labor scholar James Green has argued that most labor historians have focused on union leadership rather than the rank and file, who sought greater control at the point of production. See Green, *Workers' Struggles, Past and Present;* and Kimeldorf, *Battling for American Labor.* Political scientist Aristide Zolberg (see Zolberg, "How Many Exceptionalisms?") has proposed that American workers were more similar to those in France and England, whereas the workers in Germany were the exception. Historian William E. Forbath (see Forbath, *Law and the Shaping of the American Labor Movement*) has proposed that consciousness was not the prime reason for the historical trajectory of American labor; progressive labor movements were

undermined by the state and counts. Similarly, historical sociologist Kim Voss (see Voss, *Making of American Exceptionalism*) has observed that American labor was class-conscious in the nineteenth century but became more politically conservative in the twentieth century. She concluded that American employers and the state, not labor, were different.

11. There have been individual case studies of general strikes: Friedheim, *Seattle General Strike;* O'Conner, *Revolution in Seattle;* Eliel, *Waterfront and General Strikes of San Francisco;* Quinn, *Big Strike;* and D. Selvin, *Terrible Anger.* The Seattle and San Francisco general strikes have also been included as part of larger histories: see Kimeldorf, *Reds or Rackets;* Cross, *History of the Labor Movement in California;* Bernstein, *History of the American Worker;* Larrowe, *Harry Bridges;* Sales, *Seattle;* Nelson, *Workers on the Waterfront;* Raineri, *Red Angel;* Magden, *History of Seattle Waterfront Workers;* and Berner, *Seattle, 1900–1920.* Finally, they have also been included in studies of general strikes and industrywide strikes: Crook, *General Strike* and *Communism*, as well as Brecher, *Strike!*

12. For more on the methodological problems inherent in negative case comparisons, see Hamilton, "Why No Capitalism in China?"

13. Thomas Paine was not a "framer" in the sense of having written the founding documents. But he did write the pamphlet *Common Sense*, circulated in 1776, which inspired apprehensive colonists to become revolutionaries. Paine was also the secretary to the Committee of Foreign Affairs, through which he obtained loans and military assistance for America from France. Along with Benjamin Franklin, Paine contributed to the Pennsylvania constitution, which secured universal suffrage and religious freedom. When wealthy merchants organized to overturn the constitution because it allowed artisans and mechanics to vote, Paine defended its "democratic rights" in newspapers. After an electoral victory keeping the constitution, Paine was appointed as "clerk" or adviser to the Pennsylvania Assembly. In this capacity he wrote the preamble to an act passed by the assembly in 1780 for the gradual emancipation of slaves in the state, the first legislation of its kind in the United States. See Foner, *Life and Major Writings of Thomas Paine.*

14. See Grob, *Workers and Utopia*, 38–39.

15. Processes of movement continuity and abeyance are discussed in sociologist Verta Taylor's article, "Social Movement Continuity."

16. Bergquist, "Dialectics Democratic," 312.

17. See Goodwyn, *Populist Moment*, xv–xvi. For more on American populism, see Kazin, *Populist Persuasion.*

18. Laurie, *Artisans into Workers*, 12.

19. Sewell Jr., *Work and Revolution in France;* Thompson, *Making of the English Working Class;* and Calhoun, *Question of Class Struggle.*

20. See Wood, *Radicalism of the American Revolution* and *American Revolution;*

Shalhope, *Roots of Democracy;* Pocock, *Machiavellian Moment;* Bailyn, *Ideological Origins of the American Revolution* and *Origins of American Politics;* and Mathews, *Radical Politics of Thomas Jefferson.*

21. Boggs, *End of Politics,* 96.

22. Economist David Schweickart made this point in *Against Capitalism.*

23. Historian Gordon Wood has pointed out that English tenant farmers were as independent as colonial ones, despite the differences of ownership. See Wood, *Radicalism of the American Revolution,* 14.

24. Wertheimer, *We Were There,* 12–13.

25. Wood, *Radicalism of the American Revolution,* 67.

26. Wilentz, *Chants Democratic,* 28–29.

27. Laurie, *Artisans into Workers,* 48.

28. The term "republicanism" refers to dominant narratives from the early republic and is not the same as the current political orientation of the Republican Party in the United States.

29. Bailyn, *Ideological Origins of the American Revolution,* 54.

30. Wood, *Radicalism of the American Revolution,* 112.

31. Shalhope, *Roots of Democracy,* 46–48.

32. Laurie, *Artisans into Workers,* 49.

33. Wood, *Radicalism of the American Revolution,* 104–5.

34. Ibid., 105–7.

35. Huston, *Securing the Fruits of Labor,* 7.

36. In his First Annual Message to Congress in 1861 Abraham Lincoln stated: "Labor is prior to, and independent of capital. Capital is only the fruit of labor, and could never have existed if labor had not first existed. Labor is the superior of capital, and deserves much the higher consideration."

37. Mills, *Racial Contract.* Philosophy professor Charles Mills was inspired by feminist scholar Carole Pateman's analysis of the "hidden, unjust male covenant" that underlies the "sexual contract" in Western societies. See Pateman's *Sexual Contract.*

38. Wood, *Radicalism of the American Revolution,* 27.

39. Kramer, *Paine and Jefferson on Liberty.*

40. See Mathews, *Radical Politics of Thomas Jefferson,* 33–34.

41. Thomas Paine, *Agrarian Justice,* published in Foner, *Life and Major Writings of Thomas Paine,* 611.

42. Emphasis mine. Thomas Jefferson, Letter to James Madison, 1785, in Koch and Peden, *Life and Selected Writings of Thomas Jefferson,* 390.

43. Ibid.

44. Ibid., 252.

45. Ibid. The original version of the Declaration of Independence with the passage opposing slavery is in Jefferson's autobiography, edited by Koch and Peden, *Life and Selected Writings of Thomas Jefferson,* 22–26.

46. Rock et al., *American Artisans*, xiv.

47. Ibid.

48. Huston, *Securing the Fruits of Labor*.

49. Leach, *Land of Desire*.

50. Wilentz, *Chants Democratic*, 62.

51. The first instance of collective rather than individual bargaining with an employer took place in Philadelphia when the master shoemakers formed a trade agreement in 1799. These associations consisted of members who were skilled in a single craft. When an employer disregarded their demands, it usually resulted in a strike. See Rayback, *History of American Labor*.

52. For more about the emergence of the strike tactic in industrial societies, see historical sociologist Charles Tilly's *From Mobilization to Revolution*.

53. Bruce Laurie, "Spavined Ministers, Lying Toothpullers, and Buggering Priests: Third Partyism and the Search for Security in the Antebellum North," in Rock et al., *American Artisans*, 99.

54. Roediger, *Wages of Whiteness*, 21.

55. Ibid. See also Roediger, *Towards the Abolition of Whiteness*.

56. See Hietala, *Manifest Design;* and Horsman, *Race and Manifest Destiny*.

57. See Wilentz, *Chants Democratic*, 14–15.

58. Ibid., 166.

59. Laurie, *Artisans into Workers*, 67.

60. Ibid., 54.

61. See Teresa Murphy's "The Petitioning of Artisans and Operatives: Means and Ends in the Struggle for a Ten Hour Day," in Rock et al., *American Artisans*, 77–97.

62. Laurie, *Artisans into Workers*, 51–52.

63. Ibid., 11.

64. At a National Trade Union convention cooperatives were proposed as a way of "restructuring productive relations to maintain workplace control as early as 1836" (see Voss, *Making of American Exceptionalism*, 33).

65. Grob, *Workers and Utopia*, 6.

66. Powderly, *Thirty Years of Labor*, 48–49.

67. Grob, *Workers and Utopia*, 31.

68. Voss, *Making of American Exceptionalism*, 83–84.

69. Ibid., 81.

70. Powderly, *Thirty Years of Labor*, 233–34.

71. Most analysts have moved away from conceptualizing national cultures as universal and static systems. For a nuanced analysis of how political and "knowledge cultures" shape understandings of national citizenship, see Somers, "Privatization of Citizenship," as well as her publication "What's Political or Cultural about Political Culture and the Public Sphere?"

72. This book employs a semiotic approach (that is, the study of signs) to culture. The more common usage of the concept "sign" is derived from French linguist Ferdinand de Saussure's model; see Bally and Secheehaye, *Course in General Linguistics*, which has been expanded to include all forms of semiotic signs. The sign consists of a signifier (the material form) and a signified (the meaning elicited through the form). For more on the material and semiotic nature of culture, see Vološinov, *Marxism and the Philosophy of Language*, and Gottdiener, *Postmodern Semiotics*.

73. The term "industrial democracy" was used by labor organizations that sought ownership and management of industries but also by the Wilson administration to promote the production of war materials. In the case of the Wilson administration, the term primarily referred to collective bargaining only. See McCartin, *Labor's Great War*, and Lichtenstein and Harris, *Industrial Democracy in America*.

74. See Swindler, "Culture in Action."

75. Sources used to identify political orientations in the Seattle case include espionage reports from the collections of Broussais C. Beck, which detail conversations among union members in Seattle, from 1918 to 1920. The content of these reports was corroborated with records from the IWW, meeting minutes from the King County Central Labor Council, interviews with general strike participants found in the Papers of Robert Friedheim, the unpublished autobiography of general strike participant Hulet M. Wells *(I Wanted to Work)*, as well as excerpts from the daily labor newspaper the *Seattle Union Record* during 1919. Sources were obtained through the Manuscripts & Archives Division and Special Collections of the University of Washington Libraries in Seattle. Political orientations in the San Francisco case were constructed from letters, flyers, and strike bulletins from the International Longshoremen's Association, International Labor Defense, the Marine Workers Industrial Union, the Communist Party, and the *Waterfront Worker* newsletter, written by "rank & file longshoremen" in 1933 and 1934. These sources were available through the International Longshoremen's and Warehousemen's Union Library in San Francisco. The Bancroft Library at the University of California–Berkeley provided letters, IWW leaflets, radio addresses of ILA leaders, oral histories of participants in both general strikes, as well as the Communist Party's newsletter, the *Western Worker*.

76. Chiles, "War on the Waterfront," 17.

77. ILA, July 20, 1934, radio address, KGGC, San Francisco, ILWU Library.

78. The rejection of state control and centralized planning was not the same as seeking to change laws that privileged employer and corporate rights over those of producers.

79. ILWU commitment to political and public issues continued through the twentieth century. At the height of the cold war the union sent delegates to the

Soviet Union and Cuba. In the 1960s the union declared opposition to the Vietnam War, and by the 1980s it had engaged in direct action to protest apartheid in South Africa. Some women were working as longshorepersons by the 1990s, and during that decade the union's name changed to the International Longshore and Warehouse Union.

80. The implementation of inclusion varied with labor organizations and geographical location, a topic I discuss more fully in chapters two and three.

81. The method of difference was used as a heuristic guide to identify salient conditions in general strike trajectories. See Ragin, *Comparative Method.*

2 "A NEW POWER AND A NEW WORLD"

The chapter epigraph comes from the History Committee of the General Strike Committee, *Seattle General Strike,* 2.

1. Sales, *Seattle: Past to Present,* 35.

2. Voss, *Making of American Exceptionalism,* 83.

3. Morgan, *Skid Road.*

4. Schwantes, "Leftward Tilt on the Pacific Slope," 25.

5. Goodwyn, *Populist Moment.*

6. Dembo, "History of the Washington State Labor Movement," 27.

7. Debs, *Writings and Speeches of Eugene V. Debs,* 112.

8. Spann, *Brotherly Tomorrows,* 245.

9. Laurie, *Artisans into Workers,* 163.

10. Friedheim and Friedheim, "Seattle Labor Movement," 147.

11. Dubofsky, "Origins of Western Working Class Radicalism," 47.

12. Schwantes, "Leftward Tilt on the Pacific Slope," 30.

13. Dubofsky, "Origins of Western Working Class Radicalism." See also Foner, *History of the Labor Movement in the United States,* vol. 4, *Industrial Workers of the World,* 14–18.

14. Foner, *History of the Labor Movement in the United States,* vol. 4, 19.

15. Foster later became a communist. See Ford and Foster, *Syndicalism.*

16. Amdur, *Syndicalist Legacy.*

17. Dubofsky, *We Shall Be All,* 91; Foner, *History of the Labor Movement in the United States,* vol. 4, *Industrial Workers of the World,* 22. For more on the political orientation of the IWW, see Tyler, *Rebels in the Woods,* and Kornbluh, *Rebel Voices.*

18. Brooks, *American Syndicalism,* 64.

19. IWW, *The Industrial Worker,* May 4, 1919.

20. Ibid.

21. Ibid.

22. Wells, *I Wanted to Work,* 2, 4–5.

23. Berner, *Seattle, 1900–1920*, 169.

24. Ibid.

25. Dembo, "History of the Washington State Labor Movement," 188.

26. McCartin, *Labor's Great War*, 13.

27. Short, *History of the Activities of Seattle Labor Movement*, 1.

28. Ibid., 1–2.

29. Ault is quoted in Friedheim, *Seattle General Strike*, 148.

30. Ibid., 147.

31. Seattle Central Labor Council Minutes of King County, Washington, September 4, 1918.

32. O'Connell, "*Seattle Union Record*, 1918–1928," 5.

33. Perlman, *Theory of the Labor Movement*, 72.

34. These three factions were first identified in Friedheim, *Seattle General Strike*.

35. Strong, *I Change Worlds*, 7.

36. The IWW was organized in 1905 at a Chicago convention attended by both anarcho-syndicalists and socialists.

37. Gottdiener, *Postmodern Semiotics*, 24.

38. Berner, *Seattle, 1900–1920*, 63.

39. Ibid., 238.

40. Dembo, "History of the Washington State Labor Movement," 188.

41. Hoffman and Webb, "Police Response to Labor Radicalism in Portland and Seattle," 349–50.

42. American Protective League, "The Minute Men: Constitution and Bylaws," Accession No. 4288, Box 1, Folder 1, 2–3, University of Washington Libraries, Seattle.

43. Winslow, "Decline of Socialism in Washington," 6.

44. Hoffman and Webb, "Police Response to Labor Radicalism in Portland and Seattle," 357–58.

45. Berner, *Seattle, 1900–1920*, 248.

46. Ibid., 252–53.

47. Selvin, "Labor Union Rioters in Seattle," 6, 8.

48. *Seattle Union Record*, January 15, 1919.

49. Editorial [Oswald Garrison Villard], "The Revolt of the Rank and File," *The Nation*, October 25, 1919, 109.

50. McCartin, *Labor's Great War*, 95.

51. Montgomery, *Worker's Control in America;* Tomlins, *The State, and the Unions;* and McCartin, *Labor's Great War*.

52. *Seattle Union Record*, January 21, 1919.

53. *Seattle Union Record*, February 8, 1919.

54. Freidheim, *Seattle General Strike*, 67.

55. Berner, *Seattle General Strike, 1900–1920*, 278.

56. Freidheim, *Seattle General Strike,* 60, 61.

57. Fitch, "Labor Feels Its Muscle," 695.

58. *Seattle Union Record,* January 27, 1919.

59. Morgan, *Skid Road,* 200.

60. Freidheim, "Prologue to a General Strike," 139.

61. *Seattle Union Record,* January 31, 1919.

62. Sale, *Seattle, Past to Present,* 128.

63. *Seattle Union Record,* January 29, 1919.

64. Berner, *Seattle, 1900–1920,* 279.

65. *Seattle Union Record,* January 30, 1919.

66. *Seattle Union Record,* January 23, 1919.

67. Dembo, "History of the Washington State Labor Movement," 198.

68. Freidheim, *Seattle General Strike,* 82.

69. O'Conner, *Revolution in Seattle,* 129.

70. Strong, *I Change Worlds,* 76.

71. Ibid., 72.

72. Berner (in *Seattle, 1900–1920*) has stated that the moderate labor leaders were away and therefore unable to put the brakes on the general strike resolution. Yet O'Conner (in *Revolution in Seattle*) has argued that the radical unionists were the ones most interested in the Mooney case and were in Chicago. This meant that the members who attended the union meeting in Seattle and approved the strike resolution were the moderates and conservatives.

73. *Seattle Union Record,* January 30, 1919.

74. Morgan, *Skid Road,* 201.

75. Berner, *Seattle, 1900–1920,* 289.

76. *Seattle Union Record,* February 9, 1919.

77. D. Frank, *Purchasing Power.*

78. See Greenwald, "Working Class Feminism and the Family Wage Ideal."

79. See D. Frank, *Purchasing Power,* for an in-depth account of these activities in Seattle following the general strike.

80. Strong was well respected by the IWW because she had written some editorials in their defense. Ron Magden, interview with author, Seattle, 1994.

81. History Committee of the General Strike Committee, *Seattle General Strike,* 38.

82. Ibid., 285.

83. Capitalized words are in the original. Strong, "Who Knows Where" column, *Seattle Union Record,* February 4, 1919, 1.

84. O'Conner, *Revolution in Seattle.*

85. History Committee of the General Strike Committee, *Seattle General Strike;* Berner, *Seattle, 1900–1920,* 287.

86. Friedheim, *Seattle General Strike,* 124.

87. Morgan, *Skid Road,* 212.

88. Berner, *Seattle, 1900–1920*, 289.

89. SCLC *Strike Bulletin,* issued by the Publicity Committee of the General Strike Committee and the Metal Trades Strike Committee, February 7, 1919, Manuscripts & Archives Division, University of Washington Libraries, Seattle, 1.

90. Ibid.

91. Morgan, *Skid Road,* 212.

92. Strong, *I Change Worlds,* 82.

93. Friedheim, *Seattle General Strike,*134–35.

94. Berner, *Seattle, 1900–1920,* 290–91.

95. Sale, *Seattle, Past to Present,* 131.

96. Short, *History of the Activities of Seattle Labor Movement,* 8.

97. Berner, *Seattle, 1900–1920,* 292.

98. Freidheim, *Seattle General Strike,* 153.

99. Morgan, *Skid Road,* 214.

100. Rosenthal, "Nothing Moved but the Tide," 53, note 39.

101. Berner, *Seattle, 1900–1920,* 294.

102. Ibid., 298.

103. Rosenthal, "Nothing Moved but the Tide," 53, note 36.

104. Friedheim, *Seattle General Strike,* 162.

105. The available data indicate that "wages, hours and working conditions all show post-strike Seattle workers doing as well or better than those in the average city in the United States despite a severe depression." See Rosenthal, "Nothing Moved but the Tide," 49.

106. Strong, *I Change Worlds,* 84.

3 "TO ORGANIZE AND CONTROL THE JOB"

The chapter epigraph is from an address delivered by Ivan F. Cox, Secretary of Local 38-79, ILA. Radio Transcript, Station KGGC, July 19, 1934, ILWU Library.

1. The San Francisco general strike emerged out of a coastwide maritime strike. The focus in this chapter is primarily on events in San Francisco. For more extensive coverage of the coastwide maritime strike, see the studies cited throughout this chapter and those cited in chapter 1, note 11.

2. For excellent research documenting occupational interchange and the syndicalist orientation of West Coast maritime workers, see Kimdeldorf, *Reds or Rackets,* and Nelson, *Workers on the Waterfront.*

3. Kimeldorf, *Reds or Rackets,* 20.

4. Pilcher, *Portland Longshoremen,* 5.

5. Ibid., 40.

6. Nelson, *Workers on the Waterfront,* 65–66.

7. Chiles, "War on the Waterfront," 32.

8. Berner, *Seattle, 1900–1920*, 75.

9. Ibid., 48.

10. Magden, *History of Seattle Waterfront Workers*, 150.

11. Ibid.

12. Chiles, "War on the Waterfront," 88.

13. Ibid., 149.

14. Bernstein, *History of the American Worker*, 217.

15. Magden, *History of Seattle Waterfront Workers*, 202.

16. *Waterfront Worker*, January 29, 1934, ILWU Library.

17. Quinn, *Big Strike*, 40.

18. The quotation from Mitch Slobodek is cited in Larrowe, *Harry Bridges*, 13.

19. Ibid., 16.

20. *Waterfront Worker*, February 26, 1934, ILWU Library.

21. Chiles, "War on the Waterfront," 81, note 4.

22. *Waterfront Worker*, March 22, 1934, ILWU Library.

23. Sam Darcy, "Great West Coast Maritime Strike," 65.

24. Nelson, *Workers on the Waterfront*, 79.

25. Kimeldorf, *Reds or Rackets*.

26. Revels Cayton, interview with the author, San Francisco, 1993.

27. Chiles, "War on the Waterfront," 84.

28. Cayton, interview with the author.

29. After the NRA hearing in November 1933, President Roosevelt refused to sign the new code. An assistant secretary of commerce later explained that a shipping contract would run afoul of treaties with foreign nations whose ships used American ports; see Larrowe, *Harry Bridges*, 17.

30. *Waterfront Worker*, February 12, 1934, ILWU Library.

31. Chiles, "War on the Waterfront," 97.

32. Darcy, "Great West Coast Maritime Strike."

33. The term "employers" is used loosely here to identify the Waterfront Employers Union. In 1914 the Waterfront Employers Association was organized in the maritime industry. By February 1915, West Coast employers formed the Federation of Waterfront Employers Union. Participants included officials from "steamship lines, stevedore companies, and the Chambers of Commerce." Magden, *History of Seattle Waterfront Workers*, 78.

34. Ibid., 201.

35. Bernstein, *History of the American Worker*, 262.

36. Larrowe, *Harry Bridges*, 27.

37. Ibid., 27–28.

38. Bernstein, *History of the American Worker*, 262.

39. D. Selvin, *Terrible Anger*, 88.

40. Eliel, *Waterfront and General Strikes of San Francisco*, 19.

41. Ibid., 17.

42. Kimeldorf, *Reds or Rackets*, 146.

43. Quoted from *C. L. Dellums, President. Sleeping Car Porters Union*, Regional Oral History Project, Berkeley, California, cited in Chiles, "War on the Waterfront," 121.

44. Ibid., 122.

45. Raineri, *Red Angel*, 69.

46. From the ILD's Statement of Purpose, cited in Raineri, *Red Angel*, 25.

47. Ibid., 59.

48. Interview with Karl Yoneda, cited in Chiles, "War on the Waterfront," 110.

49. ILWU, *ILWU Story*, 18.

50. Eliel, *Waterfront and General Strikes of San Francisco*, 22.

51. Ibid., 24–25.

52. Magden, *History of Seattle Waterfront Workers*, 210.

53. ILWU, *ILWU Story*, 18.

54. Quinn, *Big Strike*, 52.

55. Ibid., 69.

56. Larrowe, *Harry Bridges*, 49.

57. Ibid., 32.

58. Quinn, *Big Strike*, 57.

59. Ibid., 73.

60. Larrowe, *Harry Bridges*, 52.

61. Ibid., 72.

62. Ibid., 74.

63. Eliel, *Waterfront and General Strikes of San Francisco*, 63.

64. Larrowe, *Harry Bridges*, 56.

65. Bernstein, *History of the American Worker*, 270.

66. ILA Radio Address, KGGC, San Francisco, California, July 19, 1934, ILWU Library.

67. Quinn, *Big Strike*, 88–89.

68. Dunne, *Great San Francisco General Strike.*

69. Eliel, *Waterfront and General Strikes of San Francisco*, 79.

70. Publicity Committee of Local 38-79, *Strike Bulletin*, No. 5, July 2, 1934, 1–2, ILWU Library.

71. Bernstein, *History of the American Worker*, 272.

72. Quinn, *Big Strike*, 104–5.

73. Ibid., 107.

74. Publicity Committee of Local 38-79, *Strike Bulletin*, No. 11, July 3, 1934, ILWU Library.

75. Quinn, *Big Strike*, 116.

76. Raineri, *Red Angel*, 73.

77. Quinn, *Big Strike*, 120.

78. Ibid.

79. Ibid.

80. Ibid., 128.

81. Eliel, *Waterfront and General Strikes of San Francisco*, 128.

82. Cayton, interview with the author, San Francisco, 1993.

83. Bernstein, *History of the American Worker*, 283.

84. Larrowe, *Harry Bridges*, 62.

85. D. Selvin, *Terrible Anger*, 168–69.

86. Letter to the NLB from M. W. Lewis, H. Bridges, Cliff Thurston, and J. Finnegan, July 15, 1934, ILWU Library, San Francisco.

87. Quinn, *Big Strike*, 138.

88. Ibid., 148–49.

89. Chamber of Commerce representative James Moffett told Marvyn H. McIntryre, assistant secretary to the president of the United States, about his conversation with Kingsbury. See D. Selvin, *Terrible Anger*, 172–73.

90. Ibid., 86.

91. Larrowe, *Harry Bridges*, 83.

92. Quinn, *Big Strike*.

93. *Waterfront Worker*, August 28, 1934, ILWU Library.

94. Publicity Committee of Local 38-79, *Strike Bulletin*, No. 24, July 21, 1934, ILWU Library.

95. Larrowe, *Harry Bridges*, 89.

96. Ibid.

97. Nelson, *Workers on the Waterfront*, 159.

98. *Waterfront Worker*, August 28, 1934, ILWU Library.

99. Retired African-American seaman Revels Cayton recalled that "there was a struggle [in Seattle] to try to keep the colored branch as sort of an auxiliary to the union branch, and same [in San Francisco]. . . . Well, the longshoremen said 'ain't gonna be no company union [referring to an auxiliary] and if you try to . . . [make] black guys go through that company union, we'll see that they get off that ship very quick. Let them go up to the hiring hall of the Marine Cooks and Stewarts and plug in just like us.'" Cayton, interview with the author, San Francisco, 1993.

100. Kimeldorf, *Reds or Rackets*, 11.

101. Hinkle, *Big Strike*, 96.

4 EXPLAINING GENERAL STRIKES

The chapter epigraph is from Harry Bridges, quoted in the *ILWU Special Bulletin* (Local 10), July 5, 1990, ILWU Library.

1. Kimeldorf, *Reds or Rackets.*

2. ILWU, *ILWU Story,* 9.

3. Ibid., 4–5.

4. Vrana, "New Film on Bridges Misses the Mark," 15.

5 THE MAKING OF MORAL CERTITUDE

The chapter epigraph is from Letter to Samuel Kercheval, 1816, "Thomas Jefferson on Politics & Government," available online at etext.virginia.edu/jefferson/quotations/jeffcont.htm. Accessed in August 2005.

1. Fantasia, *Cultures of Solidarity.*

2. V. I. Lenin argued that "class political consciousness can be brought to the workers only from without, that is, only from the outside of the economic struggle, from the outside of the sphere of relations between workers and employers" (see Lenin, *What Is to Be Done?,* 98).

3. Fantasia, *Cultures of Solidarity,* 236.

4. Ibid., 17.

5. See Kimeldorf, *Battling for American Labor.*

6. Sewell, *Work and Revolution in France;* Calhoun, *Question of Class Struggle;* and Tarrow, "Mentalities, Political Cultures, and Collective Action Frames."

7. Moore, *Injustice.*

8. Ibid. In particular, see chapter one, "Recurrent Elements in Moral Codes."

9. Lakoff, *Moral Politics.*

10. Mead, *Selected Writings.*

11. An early variation of this model can be found in Gerth and Mills, *Character and Social Structure.*

12. Sewell, "Concept(s) of Culture."

13. Moore, *Injustice,* 91.

14. Davis, *Prisoners of the American Dream,* 11–12.

15. Forbath, *Law and the Shaping of the American Labor Movement,* 27.

16. Ibid., 26.

17. Schneirov, "Political Cultures and the Role of the State in Labor's Republic."

18. Ibid.

19. Voss, *Making of American Exceptionalism.*

20. Fitch, "Labor Feels Its Muscle," 695.

21. Sewell, *Work and Revolution in France,* 276.

22. Brissenden, *I.W.W.,* 29.

23. Laurie, *Artisans into Workers*, 12.

24. IWW, *Industrial Worker*, May 4, 1919, 2.

25. Golden, "Historical Memory and Ideological Orientations," 7.

26. For a discussion of the importance of challenging discrimination in social movements, see Clawson, *Next Upsurge*.

BIBLIOGRAPHY

Amdur, Kathryn E. 1986. *Syndicalist Legacy: Trade Unions and Politics in Two French Cities in the Era of World War I.* Urbana: University of Illinois Press.

American Protective League. 1919. "The Minute Men: Constitution and Bylaws." University of Washington Libraries, Seattle.

Ault, Harry E. B. 1920–21. *American Civil Liberties Union Weekly Report on Civil Liberties Situation 1920–1921.* University of Washington Libraries, Seattle.

———. 1921–23. *Collection Correspondence Incoming, Strong Anna Louise 1921–1923.* University of Washington Libraries, Seattle.

Bailyn, Bernard. 1967. *The Ideological Origins of the American Revolution.* Cambridge: Harvard University Press.

———. 1968. *The Origins of American Politics.* New York: Vintage Books.

Bally, C., and A. Secheehaye, eds. 1966. *Course in General Linguistics.* New York: McGraw Hill.

Beck, Broussais C. 1919. "Papers, Associated Industries of Seattle Cooperative Food Products Assn. Broadsheets." University of Washington Libraries, Seattle.

Bergquist, Charles. 1994. "Dialectics Democratic: Essays on Labor and U.S. Latin American Relations." Paper presented at the Center for Comparative Research Colloquium. University of California, Davis.

Berner, Richard C. 1991. *Seattle, 1900–1920: From Boomtown, Urban Turbulence, to Restoration.* Seattle: Charles Press.

Bernstein, Irving. 1970. *A History of the American Worker, 1933–1941: The Turbulent Years.* Boston: Houghton Mifflin.

Bing, Alexander. 1921. *War-Time Strikes and Their Adjustments.* New York: E. P. Dutton.

Block, Fred. 1996. *The Vampire State: And Other Myths and Fallacies about the U.S. Economy*. New York: New Press.

Boggs, Carl. 2000. *The End of Politics: Corporate Power and the Decline of the Public Sphere*. New York: Guilford Press.

Brecher, Jeremy. 1997. *Strike!* Boston: South End Press.

Brissenden, Paul F. 1919. *The I.W.W: A Study of American Syndicalism*. New York: Russel and Russel, Inc.

Brooks, John Grahm. 1970 [1913]. *American Syndicalism: The IWW*. New York: Da Capo Press.

Calhoun, Craig. 1982. *The Question of Class Struggle: Social Foundations of Popular Radicalism during the Industrial Revolution*. Chicago: University of Chicago Press.

Cayton, Revels. 1993. Interview with author. April 1993. ILWU Library, San Francisco.

Chiles, Frederic. 1981. "War on the Waterfront: The Struggles of the San Francisco Longshoremen, 1851–1934." Ph.D. dissertation. University of California, Santa Barbara.

Clawson, Dan. 2003. *The Next Upsurge: Labor and the New Social Movements*. Ithaca, N.Y.: Cornell University Press.

Common, John. 1918–35. *The History of the Labor Movement in the United States*. 4 vols. New York: MacMillan.

Communist Party. 1934. *Western Worker*. CP, District #13, San Francisco. ILWU Library.

Crook, Wilfred. 1931. *The General Strike: A Study of Labor's Tragic Weapon in Theory and Practice*. Chapel Hill: University of North Carolina Press.

———. 1960. *Communism and the General Strike*. Hamden, Conn.: Shoe String Press.

Cross, Ira B. 1935. *A History of the Labor Movement in California*. Berkeley: University of California Press.

Darcy, Sam. 1934. "The Great West Coast Maritime Strike." *The Communist*, July 13, 664–86. ILWU Library, San Francisco.

Davis, Mike. 1986. *Prisoners of the American Dream: Politics and Economy in the History of the American Working Class*. London: Verso.

Debs, Eugene. 1948. *Writings and Speeches of Eugene V. Debs*. New York: Hermitage Press.

Dembo, Jonathan. 1978. "A History of the Washington State Labor Movement, 1885–1935." Ph.D. dissertation. University of Washington.

Dubofsky, Melvyn. 2000. "The Origins of Western Working Class Radicalism." In *Hard Work: The Making of Labor History*. Urbana: University of Illinois Press, 41–65.

————.1969. *We Shall Be All*. Chicago: Quadrangle Books.

Dunne, William. 1934. *The Great San Francisco General Strike*. New York: Workers Library Publishers.

Eliel, Paul. 1934. *The Waterfront and General Strikes of San Francisco, 1934: A Brief History*. San Francisco: Industrial Association of San Francisco.

Fantasia, Rick. 1988. *Cultures of Solidarity: Consciousness, Action, and Contemporary American Workers*. Berkeley: University of California Press.

Fitch, John. 1919. "Labor Feels Its Muscle." *The Survey* (February 15): 695–96.

Foner, Phillip. 1976. *History of the Labor Movement in the United States*. Vol. 4, *The Industrial Workers of the World*. New York: International Publishers.

————. 1980. *History of the Labor Movement in the United States*. Vol. 5, *The AFL in the Progressive Era, 1910–1915*. New York: International Publishers.

————, ed. 1993. *The Life and Major Writings of Thomas Paine*. New Jersey: Replica Books, a division of Baker and Taylor.

Forbath, William E. 1991. *Law and the Shaping of the American Labor Movement*. Cambridge: Harvard University Press.

Ford, Earl, and William Foster. 1990 [1912]. *Syndicalism*. Chicago: Charles H. Kerr Publishing.

Frank, Dana. 1994. *Purchasing Power: Consumer Organizing, Gender, and the Seattle Labor Movement, 1919–1929*. Cambridge: Cambridge University Press.

Frank, Thomas. 2004. *What's the Matter with Kansas? How the Conservatives Won the Heart of America*. New York: Henry Holt Company.

Friedheim, Robert L. 1964. *The Seattle General Strike*. Seattle: University of Washington Press.

————. 1965. "Prologue to a General Strike: The Seattle Shipyard Strike of 1919." *Labor History* 4 (spring): 121–42.

Friedheim, Robert. 1946–47. "Interviews with Seattle General Strike Participants." Papers of Robert Friedheim. University of Washington Libraries, Seattle.

Friedheim, Robert L., and Robin Friedheim. 1964. "The Seattle Labor Movement, 1919–20." *Pacific Northwest Quarterly* (October): 146–69.

Gerth, Hans, and C. W. Mills. 1953. *Character and Social Structure: The Psychology of Social Institutions*. New York: Harcourt, Brace & World.

Goldblatt, Louis. *Oral History: Louis Goldblatt: Working Class Leader in the ILWU, 1935–1977*. Bancroft Library, University of California, Berkeley.

Golden, Miriam. 1988. "Historical Memory and Ideological Orientations in the Italian Workers' Movement." *Politics & Society* 16 (1) (March): 1–34.

Goodwyn, Lawrence. 1978. *The Populist Moment: A Short History of the Agrarian Revolt in America*. Oxford: Oxford University Press.

Gordon, David M., et al. 1988. *Segmented Work, Divided Workers: The Historical*

Transformation of Labor in the United States. Cambridge: Cambridge University Press.

Gottdiener, M. 1995. *Postmodern Semiotics: Material Culture and the Forms of Postmodern Life.* Oxford: Blackwell.

Green, James, ed. 1993. *Workers' Struggles, Past and Present: A "Radical American" Reader.* Philadelphia: Temple University Press.

Greenwald, Maurine Weiner. 2001. "Working Class Feminism and the Family Wage Ideal." In *Women in Pacific Northwest History.* Edited by Karen Blair. Seattle: University of Washington Press, 94–134.

Grob, Gerald. 1961. *Workers and Utopia: A Study of Ideological Conflict in the American Labor Movement, 1865–1900.* Chicago: Quadrangle Books.

Hamilton, Gary. 1985. "Why No Capitalism in China? Negative Questions in Historical and Comparative Research." *Journal of Developing Societies* 1: 187–211.

Hietala, Thomas. 2003. *Manifest Design: American Exceptionalism and Empire.* Ithaca, N.Y.: Cornell University Press.

Hinkle, Warren. 1985. *The Big Strike: A Pictorial History of the 1934 San Francisco General Strike.* Virginia City, Nev.: Silver Dollar Books.

History Committee of the General Strike Committee. 1919. *The Seattle General Strike: An Account of What Happened in Seattle, and Especially the Seattle Labor Movement, during the General Strike. February 6–11, 1919.* Seattle: Seattle Union Record Publishing Company.

Hoffman, Dennis, and Vincent Webb. 1986. "Police Response to Labor Radicalism in Portland and Seattle, 1913–19." *Oregon Historical Quarterly* (winter): 341–66.

Horsman, Reginald. 1986. *Race and Manifest Destiny: Origins of American Racial Anglo-Saxonism.* Cambridge: Harvard University Press.

Huston, James L. 1998. *Securing the Fruits of Labor: The American Concept of Wealth Distribution, 1765–1900.* Baton Rouge: Louisiana State University Press.

Industrial Workers of the World (IWW). 1919. *The Industrial Worker.* University of Washington Libraries, Seattle.

International Longshoremen's Association. 1934. Radio transcript delivered by Ivan F. Cox, secretary of Local 38-79, ILA. Station KGGC, July 19. ILWU Library, San Francisco.

————.1934. Women's Auxiliary Flyer. ILWU Library, San Francisco.

International Longshoremen's and Warehousemen's Union (ILWU). 1963. *The ILWU Story: Three Decades of Militant Unionism.* 2d edition, revised. San Francisco: ILWU Information Department.

Jefferson, Thomas. "Thomas Jefferson on Politics & Government." University of Virginia. Available online at etext.virginia.edu/jefferson/quotations/jeffcont.htm. Accessed in May 2005.

Johnson, Victoria. 2000. "The Cultural Foundation of Resources, the Resource Foundation of Political Cultures: Explaining the Outcomes of Two General Strikes." *Politics and Society* 28 (3): 331–65.

Joint Strike Committee of the International Seamen's Union of America, Pacific Coast District. 1934. *Strike Bulletins*. International Seamen's Union of America, ILWU Library, San Francisco.

Kazin, Michael. 1995. *The Populist Persuasion: An American History*. New York: Basic Books.

Kimeldorf, Howard. 1988. *Reds or Rackets: The Making of Radical and Conservative Unions on the Waterfront*. Berkeley: University of California Press.

———. 1999. *Battling for American Labor: Wobblies, Craft Workers, and the Making of the Union Movement*. Berkeley: University of California Press.

Koch, Adrienne, and William Peden, eds. 1972. *The Life and Selected Writings of Thomas Jefferson*. New York: Random House.

Kornbluh, Joyce, ed. 1964. *Rebel Voices: An I.W.W. Anthology*. Ann Arbor: University of Michigan Press.

Kramer, Lloyd, ed. 1994. *Paine and Jefferson on Liberty*. New York: Continuum.

Lakoff, George. 2002. *Moral Politics: How Liberals and Conservatives Think*. Chicago: University of Chicago Press.

———. 2004. *Don't Think of an Elephant: Know Your Values and Frame the Debate*. White River Junction, Vt.: Chelsea Green Publishing.

Lannon, Albert. 1993. "Oakland and the General Strike of 1946 Remembered." *East Bay Labor Journal* (November–December).

Larrowe, Charles P. 1972. *Harry Bridges: The Rise and Fall of Radical Labor in the United States*. New York: Lawrence Hill and Co.

Larry, Issac W. 2000. "Class Conflict." *Encyclopedia of Violence, Peace, Conflict*. Vol. 1, 297–317.

Laslett, John, and Seymour Martin Lipset. 1974. *Failure of a Dream: Essays in the History of American Socialism*. New York: Anchor Books.

Laurie, Bruce. 1997. *Artisans into Workers: Labor in Nineteenth-Century America*. Urbana: University of Illinois Press.

Leach, William. 1994. *Land of Desire: Merchants, Power, and the Rise of a New American Culture*. New York: Vintage Books.

Lenin, V. I. 1973 [1902]. *What Is to Be Done? Burning Questions of Our Movement*. Beijing [Peking]: Foreign Languages Press.

Lewis, M. W., H. Bridges, Cliff Thurston, and J. Finnegan. 1934. Letter to National Longshoremen's Board. July 15. ILWU Library, San Francisco.

Lichtenstein, Nelson, and Howell John Harris. 1996. *Industrial Democracy in America: The Ambiguous Promise*. Cambridge: Cambridge University Press.

Lipset, Seymour Martin. 1996. *American Exceptionalism: A Double Edged Sword*. New York: W. W. Norton.

Lipsitz, George. 1994. *Rainbow at Midnight: Labor and Culture in the 1940s.* Chicago: University of Illinois Press.

Magden, Ronald E. 1991. *A History of Seattle Waterfront Workers, 1884–1934.* Seattle: ILWU Local 19 and the Washington Commission.

Marine Workers Industrial Union. 1934. *Ryan Sells Out I.L.A.* Flyer. ILWU Library, San Francisco.

Mathews, Richard K. 1984. *The Radical Politics of Thomas Jefferson.* Lawrence: University of Kansas Press.

McCartin, Joseph A. 1997. *Labor's Great War: The Struggle for Industrial Democracy and the Origins of Modern American Labor Relations, 1912–1921.* Chapel Hill: University of North Carolina Press.

Mead, George Herbert. 1964. *Selected Writings.* Chicago: University of Chicago Press.

Mills, Charles. 1997. *The Racial Contract.* Ithaca, N.Y.: Cornell University Press.

Montgomery, David. 1979. *Worker's Control in America.* Cambridge: Cambridge University Press.

Moore, Barrington. 1978. *Injustice: The Social Basis of Obedience and Revolt.* Armonk, N.Y.: M. E. Sharpe.

Morgan, Murray. 1991. *Skid Road: An Informal Portrait of Seattle.* Seattle: University of Washington Press.

Nelson, Bruce. 1990. *Workers on the Waterfront: Seamen, Longshoremen, and Unionism in the 1930s.* Urbana: University of Illinois Press.

O'Connell, Mary Joan. 1964. "The *Seattle Union Record,* 1918–1928." Master's thesis. University of Washington.

O'Conner, Harvey. 1964. *Revolution in Seattle: A Memoir.* New York: Monthly Review Press.

Pateman, Carole. 1988. *The Sexual Contract.* Stanford, Calif.: Stanford University Press.

Perlman, Selig. 1970 [1928]. *The Theory of the Labor Movement.* New York: Augustus M. Kelley Publishers.

Pilcher, William W. 1972. *The Portland Longshoremen: A Dispersed Urban Community.* New York: Holt, Rinehart, and Winston.

Pocock, J. G. A. 1975. *The Machiavellian Moment: Florentine Political Thought and the Atlantic Republican Tradition.* Princeton, N.J.: Princeton University Press.

Powderly, Terence V. 1967 [1890]. *Thirty Years of Labor, 1859 to 1889.* New York: Augustus M. Kelly Publishers.

Publicity Committee of Local 38-79. 1934. *Strike Bulletins,* Nos. 5, 11, and 24. ILWU Library, San Francisco.

Publicity Committee of the General Strike Committee and the Metal Trades Strike Committee Central Labor Council. 1919. *Strike Bulletins.* University of Washington Libraries, Seattle.

Quinn, Mike. 1949. *The Big Strike.* New York: International Publishers.

Ragin, Charles C. 1989. *The Comparative Method: Moving beyond Qualitative and Quantitative Strategies.* Berkeley: University of California Press.

Raineri, Vivian McGuckin. 1991. *The Red Angel: The Life and Times of Elaine Black Yoneda, 1906–1988.* New York: International Publishers.

Rank and File Longshoremen. 1934. *Waterfront Worker* newsletters. ILWU Library, San Francisco.

Rayback, Joseph. 1966. *A History of American Labor.* New York: Free Press.

Rock, Howard B., et al. 1995. *American Artisans: Crafting Social Identity, 1750–1850.* Baltimore, Md.: Johns Hopkins University Press.

Roediger, David. 1994. *Towards the Abolition of Whiteness: Essays on Race, Politics, and Working Class History.* New York: Verso.

———. 1991. *The Wages of Whiteness: Race and the Making of the American Working Class.* London: Verso.

Rosenthal, Rob. 1992. "Nothing Moved but the Tide: The Seattle General Strike of 1919." *Labor's Heritage* 5 (3): 36–53.

Sale, Roger. 1976. *Seattle, Past to Present.* Seattle: University of Washington Press.

San Francisco Chronicle, 1934.

Schneirov, Richard. 1991. "Political Cultures and the Role of the State in Labor's Republic: The View from Chicago, 1848–1877." *Labor History* 32 (3): 376–400.

Schwantes, Carlos. 1979. "Leftward Tilt on the Pacific Slope: Indigenous Unionism and the Struggle against AFL Hegemony in the State of Washington." *Pacific Northwest Quarterly* 70 (1): 24–34.

Schweickart, David. 1996. *Against Capitalism.* Boulder, Colo.: Westview Press.

Seattle Central Labor Council (SCLC) Minutes, King County. 1919. University of Washington Libraries, Seattle.

Seattle Star, 1919.

Seattle Times, 1919.

Seattle Union Record, 1919.

Selvin, David F. 1996. *A Terrible Anger: The 1934 Waterfront and General Strikes in San Francisco.* Detroit, Mich.: Wayne State University Press.

Selvin, Edwin, ed. 1919. "Labor Union Rioters in Seattle Call for Government's Overthrow and Start a Bolshevik Soviet." *Business Chronicle of the Pacific Northwest* 6 (8): 8–9.

Sewell, William, Jr. 1980. *Work and Revolution in France: The Language of Labor from the Old Regime to 1848.* Cambridge: Cambridge University Press.

———. 1999. "The Concept(s) of Culture." In *Beyond the Cultural Turn: New Directions in the Study of Culture and Society.* Edited by Victoria Bonnell and Lynn Hunt. Berkeley: University of California Press, 35–61.

Shalhope, Robert. 1990. *The Roots of Democracy*. Lanham, Md.: Rowman and Littlefield.

Short, W. M. 1919. *History of the Activities of Seattle Labor Movement and Conspiracy of Employers to Destroy It and Attempted Suppression of Labor's Daily Newspaper. Seattle Union Record*, 1919. University of Washington Libraries, Seattle.

Sombart, Werner. 1976. *Why Is There No Socialism in the United States?* White Plains, N.Y.: International Arts and Sciences Press.

Somers, Margaret. 1995. "What's Political or Cultural about Political Culture and the Public Sphere? Toward an Historical Sociology of Concept Formation." *Sociological Theory* 13 (2):113–44.

———. 1999. "The Privatization of Citizenship: How to Unthink a Knowledge Culture." In *Beyond the Cultural Turn: New Directions in the Study of Culture and Society*. Edited by Victoria Bonnell and Lynn Hunt. Berkeley: University of California Press, 121–61.

Spann, Edward K. 1989. *Brotherly Tomorrows: Movements for a Cooperative Society in America, 1820–1920*. New York: Columbia University Press.

Strong, Anna Louise. 1935. *I Change Worlds: The Remaking of an American*. New York: Henry Holt and Company.

Swindler, Ann. 1986. "Culture in Action: Symbols and Strategies." *American Sociological Review* 51: 273–86.

Tarrow, Sydney. 1992. "Mentalities, Political Cultures, and Collective Action Frames: Constructing Meanings through Action." In *Frontiers in Social Movement Theory*. Edited by Aldon Morris and Carol McClurg. New Haven, Conn.: Yale University Press, 174–202.

Taylor, Verta. 1989. "Social Movement Continuity: The Women's Movement in Abeyance." *American Sociological Review* 54: 761–75.

Teamsters Members for a Rank & File Movement. 1934. *The Teamster* newsletters. San Francisco, ILWU Library.

Thompson, E. P. 1966. *The Making of the English Working Class*. New York: Vintage.

Tilly, Charles. 1978. *From Mobilization to Revolution*. New York: McGraw-Hill.

Tomlins, Christopher. 1985. *The State, and the Unions: Labor Relations, Law, and the Organized Labor Movement in America, 1880–1960*. Cambridge: Cambridge University Press.

Tyler, Robert. 1967. *Rebels in the Woods: The I.W.W. in the Pacific Northwest*. Eugene: University of Oregon Press.

Vološinov, V. N. 1973. *Marxism and the Philosophy of Language*. New York: Seminar Press.

Voss, Kim. 1993. *The Making of American Exceptionalism: The Knights of Labor and Class Formation in the Nineteenth Century*. Ithaca, N.Y.: Cornell University Press.

Vrana, Gene Dennis. 1992. "New Film on Bridges Misses the Mark." *The Dispatcher,* October 15.

Wells, Hulet M. *I Wanted to Work.* Unpublished manuscript, Hulet M. Wells papers, 1909–1964. University of Washington Libraries, Seattle.

Wertheimer, Barbara Mayer. 1977. *We Were There: The Story of Working Women in America.* New York: Pantheon Press.

Wilentz, Sean. 1984. *Chants Democratic: New York City and the Rise of the American Working Class.* New York: Oxford University Press.

Winslow, Barbara. 1969. "The Decline of Socialism in Washington, 1910–1925." Master's thesis, University of Washington, University of Washington Libraries, Seattle.

Wood, Gordon. 1991. *The Radicalism of the American Revolution.* New York: Vintage Books.

———. 2003. *The American Revolution.* New York: Random House.

Zolberg, Aristide. 1986. "How Many Exceptionalisms?" In *Working-Class Formation: Nineteenth-Century Patterns in Western Europe and the United States.* Edited by Ira Katnelson and Aristide Zolberg. Princeton, N.J.: Princeton University Press.

INDEX

129; and Enlightenment, 19; and
  Jacksonians, 20; and manifest destiny, 19, 20

Darcy, Sam, 76
Davis, Mike, 122
de Barbé-Marbois, Marquis, 16
Deal, Clyde, 98
Debs, Eugene, 124
Declaration of Independence, 127;
  and Jefferson's passage opposing
  slavery, 134
Dellums, C. L., 82, 83
Department of Justice, 45
Department of Labor, 46, 66
Dispatcher, The, 115
Duncan, James, 64
Dunne,William, 91

Early Republic, 7, 12, 17, 18, 33, 126;
  and agrarian languages, 11, 119;
  and banks, 12; and culture of contradictions, 11, 15; and disinterestedness, 14; and labor theory of
  property/value, 14; and land, 123;
  and municipal price controls, 13
economy, 32; and decreased productivity, 67; and increased cost of living, 50; and increased productivity,
  39, 71
Eliel, Paul, 96
Emergency Fleet Corporation, 4, 39,
  49–50; suspended contracts of, 67
English republicanism, 11
Espionage Act, 46
Eugene, Debs, 34
Evans, George Henry, 21

Fantasia, Rick, 117
farmer-labor party, 43
Farmers Alliance, 33

Federal Employees Union, 55
Federalist No. 10, 123
Foisie, Frank, 86
Forbath, William E., 123
Forbes, John, 94
Foster, William, 36
Franklin, Benjamin, 133
free labor ideology: and artisan
  republicanism, 20; and Jackson-
  ians, 20; and merchant capi-
  talists, 21
Freidheim, Robert L., 54

General Strike Committee, 57, 64,
  98, 101; and accepted resolution,
  65; and called-off strike, 64
general strikes, 8, 54, 73; distinctive
  characteristics of, 5; San Francisco,
  88–101; Seattle, 53–65; in U.S.
  history, 5; and violation of AFL
  rules, 64

Hanson, Ole, 46, 61–62, 63, 64, 65;
  and stopped "revolution," 66
Harding, Warren, 66
Hawthorne, C. M., 40
Hearst, William Randolph, 86
History Committee of the General
  Strike Committee, 31, 57, 65, 67
Holman, Lee, 74, 77, 107; as local
  38–79 president, 80; suspension
  as Local 38–79 president, 81; and
  Executive Board, 79
Hoover, Herbert, 73
hotel maids, 55
house-painters and decorators, 55
Hull, Cordell, 100
Huston, James L., 14

ideal types, 25, 28; and political orientations, 27

identities, 30, 38, 83, 116, 125–26; class, 83, 121; collective, 119; construction of, 120; and emotional management, 119–20; institutional, 122; and moral certitude, 119; and national narratives, 126; and need fulfillment, 119; racialized and gendered, 121; and the state, 122

Industrial Association (IA), 88, 89, 94; and opening the port, 92

industrial democracy. *See* workplace democracy

industrial unionism, 26, 35–36, 41, 49, 57, 71; and ILWU, 113; and organizational logic of, 118

industrialization: in Seattle, 32; and workplace disempowerment, 118

Indians. *See* indigenous populations

indigenous populations, 19, 127

Industrial Worker, The, 126

Industrial Workers of the World (IWW), 60, 75, 76, 110, 126; and AFL, 117; and American Labor Union, 35; and anti-syndicalism bill arrests, 66; distinct from socialism, 44; and general srike, 66; influence of in Seattle, 54; and Knights of Labor, 36, 82; and metal trades union, 54, 106; motto of, 104; and Oregon logging, 71; and producerist discursive strands, 37; and racial inclusion, 82, 84; repression of, 45, 46, 65; strategy of, 40, 43; and syndicalism, 36; and West Coast maritime culture, 69. *See also* workplace democracy

International Association of Machinists, 92

International Labor Defense (ILD), 84, 95; and legal aid, 86, 100; and Prisoners Relief Fund, 85

International Longshoremen's Association (ILA), 25, 72, 86, 91, 92; African Americans as auxilary branch of, 143n99; dual authority and tensions of, 87, 97, 103; East Coast leadership of, 80, 82; and funeral procession, 96; moderate orientation of, 80–81; and new union, 74, 77; and 1919 strike, 110; and Pacific Coast District, 80; and patriarchy, 84; and racism, 72; and radio transcript, 14; strategy of, 81; women's auxilary, 84

International Longshoremen's and Warehousemen's Union (ILWU), 28, 90, 93, 103, 107, 114–15, 140; and commitment to public issues, 136; and industrial unionism, 113; Tenth Biennial Convention of, 113

International Seamen's Union, 88

Italy's invasion of Ethiopia, 26

Jacksonian Democrats, 7, 115; and culture of contradictions, 20

Jacksonian Era, 22

Japanese internment, 26

Jefferson, Thomas, 22, 30, 37, 116, 123, 131; agreement with Thomas Paine, 15; inspired movement for self-governing workshop, 6; innovation of principles, 126–29; labor theory of property/value, 14; and passage opposing slavery in Declaration of Independence, 134; and personified culture of contradictions, 17; philosophy of, 7, 12–13; and race, 19; state distribution of resources and, 8; unequal division of property in Europe and,